THE CHAMPION'S GUIDE TO MATH OLYMPIAD

For Elementary & Middle Schools

AMERICAN MATH
ACADEMY

By H. TONG, M.Ed.

Math Instructor & Olympiad Coach
www.americanmathacademy.com

AMERICAN MATH ACADEMY

THE CHAMPION'S GUIDE TO MATH OLYMPIAD

For Elementary & Middle Schools

Questions, suggestions or comments, please email: americanmathacademy@gmail.com

TABLE OF CONTENTS

BOOKS BY AMERICAN MATH ACADEMY

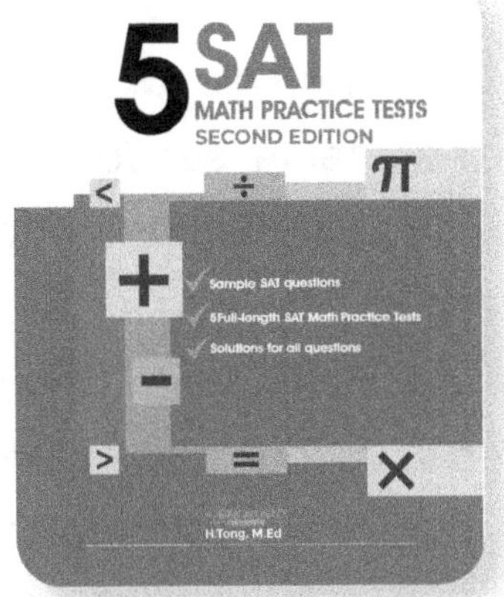

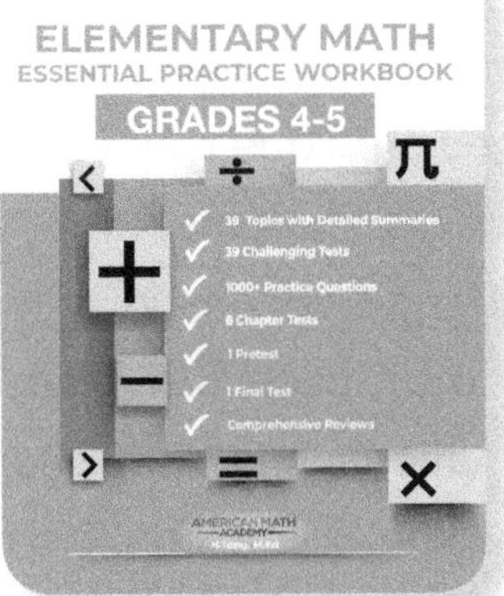

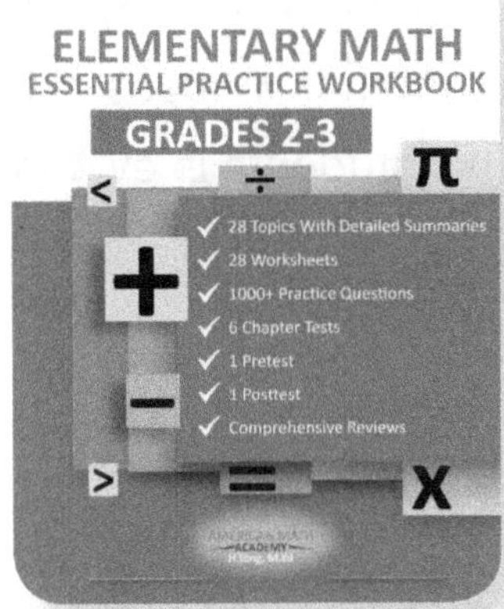

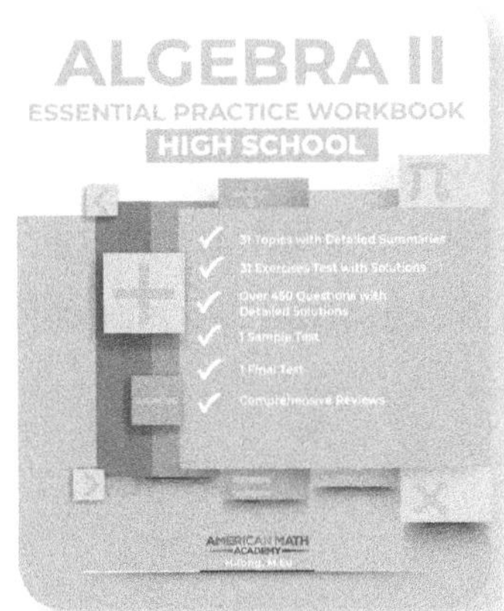

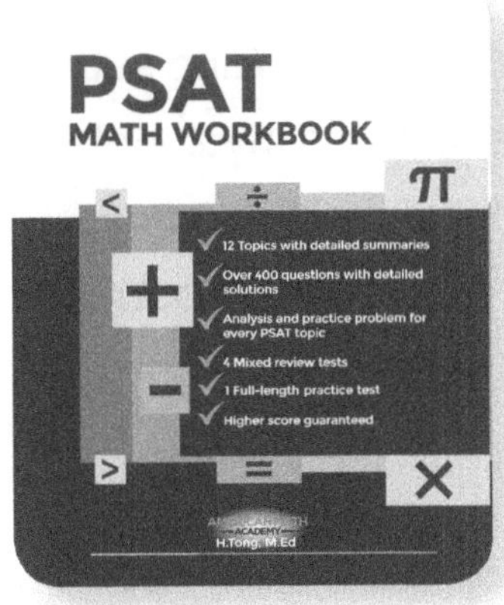

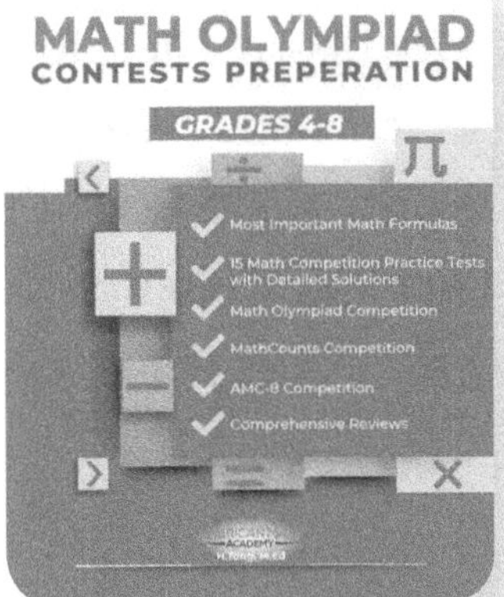

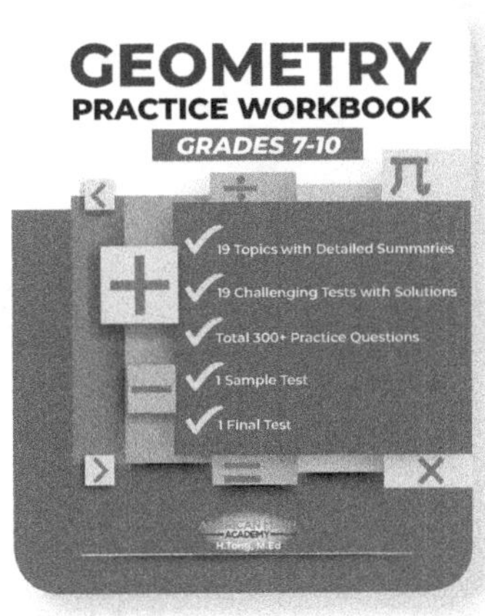

About the Author

Mr. Tong teaches at various private and public schools in both New York and New Jersey. In conjunction with his teaching, Mr. Tong developed his own private tutoring company. His company developed a unique way of ensuring their students' success on the math section of the SAT. Over the years his students, have been able to apply the knowledge and skills they've learned during their tutoring sessions in college and beyond. Mr. Tong's academic accolades make him the best candidate to teach SAT Math. He received his Master's Degree in Math Education. He has won several national and state championships in various math competitions and has taken his team to victory in the Olympiads. He has trained students for Math Counts, American Math Competition (AMC), Harvard MIT Math Tournament, Princeton Math Contest, and the National Math League, and many other events. His teaching style ensures student success. He puts great effort, and time into his students. He uses different teaching strategies to help struggling students. His dedication towards his students is evident through his student's achievements.

Acknowledgements

I would like to take the time to acknowledge the help and support of my beloved wife, my colleagues, and my students–their feedback on my book was invaluable. I would like to say an additional thank you to my dear friend Robert for his assistance in making this book complete. Without everyone's help, this book would not be the same. I dedicate this book to my precious daughter Vera and Nora who were my inspiration to take on this project.

MOST IMPORTANT MATH KEY POINTS

Natural Numbers(N)
Definition: Counting numbers starting from 1, extending upwards (1, 2, 3, 4, ...).

Whole Numbers (N_0)
Definition: Natural numbers including 0 (0, 1, 2, 3, 4, ...).

Integers (Z)
Definition: All whole numbers including negatives (-3, -2, -1, 0, 1, 2, 3, ...).

Rational Numbers (Q)
Definition: Numbers that can be expressed as the quotient of two integers (½, 0.75).

Irrational Numbers
Definition: Numbers that cannot be expressed as a simple fraction ($\sqrt{2}$, π).

Real Numbers (R)
Definition: All numbers on the continuous number line, including rational and irrational numbers.

Prime Numbers: Greater than 1, divisible only by 1 and itself.
Examples: 2, 3, 5, 7, 11, ...

Composite Numbers: have divisors other than 1 and themselves
Examples: 4, 6, 8, 9, 10, ...

Even Numbers: Divisible by 2 without aremainder.
Examples: -4, -2, 0, 2, 4, 6, ...

Odd Numbers: Not divisible by 2; dividing by 2 leaves a remainder of 1.
Examples: -3, -1, 1, 3, 5, ...

MOST IMPORTANT MATH KEY POINTS

Negative Integers: Whole numbers less than zero.

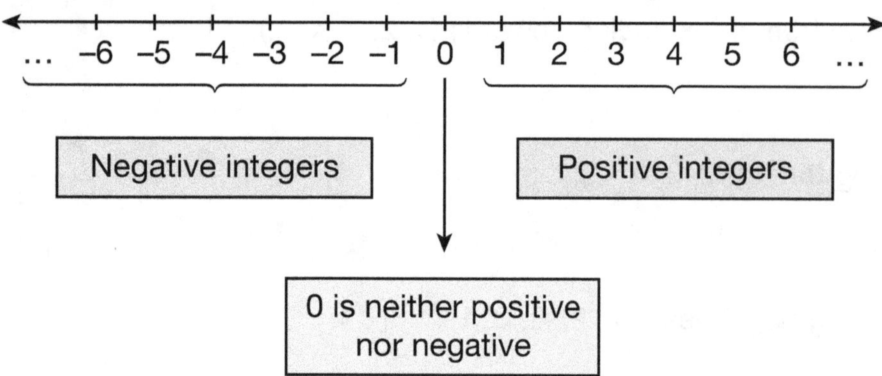

Opposites: Numbers that are the same distance from zero but on different sides of zero.

Examples:

- ✓ The opposite of 4 is −4
- ✓ The opposite of 0.6 is −0.6
- ✓ The opposite of $\frac{1}{2}$ is $-\frac{1}{2}$

Reciprocal: The reciprocal is the multiplicative inverse of a number.

- ✓ The reciprocal of $\frac{1}{2}$ is 2
- ✓ The reciprocal of $\frac{4}{3}$ is $\frac{3}{4}$
- ✓ The reciprocal of 7 is $\frac{1}{7}$

MOST IMPORTANT MATH KEY POINTS

Prime Factorization

Definition: Prime factorization is the process of expressing a composite number as the product of its prime factors.

Example: Find the prime factorization of 60.

Solution:
60 can be divided by 2 (the smallest prime number) to get 30.
30 can be divided by 2 again to get 15.
15 can be divided by 3 to get 5, which is a prime number.
Thus, the prime factorization of 60 is 2 x 2 x 3 x 5.

Least Common Multiple (LCM)
Definition: The LCM of two or more integers is the smallest positive integer that is divisible by each of the numbers without any remainder.

Example: Find the LCM of 12 and 18.

Solution:

Prime factorization of 12 is 2^2 x 3.
Prime factorization of 18 is 2 x 3^2.
LCM takes the highest power of each prime factor present in the numbers: $2^2 \times 3^2 = 4 \times 9 = 36$.
So, the LCM of 12 and 18 is 36.

Greatest Common Factor (GCF) or Greatest Common Divisor (GCD

Definition: The GCF of two or more integers is the largest positive integer that divides each of the numbers without any remainder.

Example: Find the GCF of 48 and 64.

Solution:

Prime factorization of 48 is $2^4 \times 3$.
Prime factorization of 64 is 2^6.
The GCF takes the lowest power of common prime factors: 2^4.
So, the GCF of 48 and 64 is $2^4 = 16$.

Commutative Property

For Addition: $a+b=b+a$
For Multiplication: $a \times b = b \times a$

Example (Addition): $3 + 5 = 5+3=8$
Example (Multiplication): $4 \cdot 6 = 6 \cdot 4 = 24$

Associative Property

For Addition: $(a + b) + c = a + (b + c)$
For Multiplication: $(a \cdot b) \cdot c = a \cdot (b \cdot c)$

Example (Addition): $(2+3)+4 = 2 + (3 + 4) = 9$
Example (Multiplication): $(2 \cdot 3) \cdot 4 = 2 \cdot (3 \cdot 4) = 24$

Distributive Property

Formula: $a \cdot (b + c) = a \cdot b + a \cdot c$
Example: $2 \cdot (3 + 4) = 2 \cdot 3 + 2 \cdot 4 = 6 + 8 = 14$

Identity Property
For Addition: $a + 0 = a$
For Multiplication: $a \cdot 1 = a$

Example (Addition): $7 + 0 = 7$
Example (Multiplication): $9 \cdot 1 = 9$

Inverse Property

For Addition: a + (-a) = 0
For Multiplication (for non-zero a): a · 1/a = 1

Example (Addition): 5+ (−5) = 0
Example (Multiplication): $4 \cdot \frac{1}{4} = 1$

Zero Property of Multiplication

Formula: a. 0 = 0
Example: 1 · 0=0

Property of One as an Exponent

Formula: $a^1 = a$
Example: $5^1 = 5$

Property of Zero as an Exponent

Formula: $a^0 = 1$ (given a≠0)
Example: $2^0 = 1$

Prime Number Property

Definition: A prime number is a natural number greater than 1 that has no positive divisors other than 1 and itself.
Example: 7 is a prime number because its only divisors are 1 and 7.

Composite Number Property

Definition: A composite number is a natural number greater than 1 that is not prime (i.e., it has more than two distinct positive divisors).
Example: 4 is a composite number because it has divisors 1, 2, and 4.

Proper fractions: A fraction where the numerator is less than the denominator.

Example: $\dfrac{1}{3}$

Improper fractions: A fraction where the denominator is less than the numerator.

Example: $\dfrac{3}{2}$

Mixed Fractions: When a fraction is written in the form $A\dfrac{B}{C}$.

Example: $5\dfrac{1}{2}$

Adding Fractions: If the fractions have different denominators:

    ✓ Find the smallest multiple (LCD) of both numbers

    ✓ Rewrite the fractions as equivalent fractions with the LCD as the denominator.

Key: $\dfrac{a}{b}+\dfrac{c}{b}=\dfrac{a+c}{b}$

$$\dfrac{a}{b}+\dfrac{c}{d}=\dfrac{a\cdot(d)}{b\cdot(d)}+\dfrac{c\cdot(b)}{d\cdot(b)}=\dfrac{ad+cb}{bd}$$

Subtracting Fractions: If the fractions have different denominators;

    ✓ Find the smallest multiple (LCD) of both numbers

    ✓ Rewrite the fractions as equivalent fractions with the LCD as the denominator.

Key: $\dfrac{a}{b}+\dfrac{c}{b}=\dfrac{a+c}{b}$

$$\dfrac{a}{b}+\dfrac{c}{d}=\dfrac{a\cdot(d)}{b\cdot(d)}+\dfrac{c\cdot(b)}{d\cdot(b)}=\dfrac{ad+cb}{bd}$$

Multiplying Fractions:

Key: $\dfrac{a}{b} \cdot \dfrac{c}{d} = \dfrac{a \cdot (c)}{b \cdot (d)} = \dfrac{ac}{bd}$

Step 1: Multiply the numerators

Step 2: Multiply the denominators

Step 3: Simplify the fraction if needed

Dividing Fractions:

$\dfrac{a}{b} \div \dfrac{c}{d} = \dfrac{a(d)}{b(c)} = \dfrac{ad}{bc}$

Step 1: Flip the divisor (the second franction)

Step 2: Multiply the first fraction by that reciprocal

Step 3: Simplify the fraction if needed

Scientific Notation

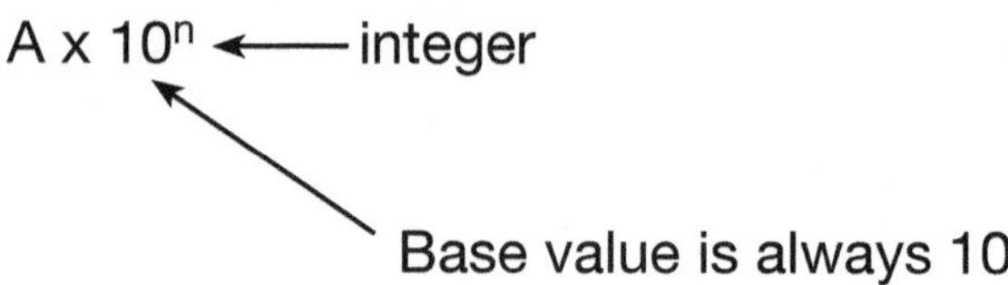

$A \times 10^n$

$1 \le |A| < 10$

A is number greater than or equal to 1 but less than 10

Algebraic Expressions

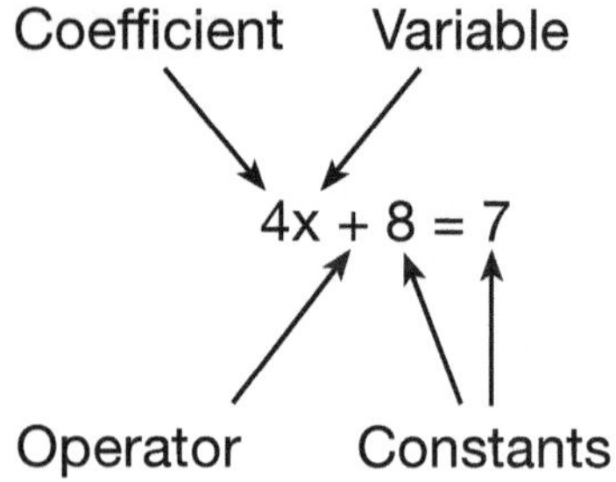

MOST IMPORTANT MATH KEY POINTS

Rounding Decimals:

✓ Identify the unit's digit

✓ Round up or down

✓ If the digit is 5 or greater, add one more.

✓ If the digit is less than 5, leave it the same.

Example: Round 68 to the nearest tens.

Solution: Keep the 6. The next digit is "8" which is 5 or more, so increase the "6" by 1 to 7. So the answer is 70.

Place Value Chart										
Millions	Hundred Thousands	Ten Thousands	Thousands	Hundreds	Tens	Ones	Decimal Point	Tenths	Hundredths	Thousandths
1	3	5	6	7	8	9	.	7	6	4
Whole Number								Decimal Number		

One million, three hundred fifty six thousand, seven hundred eighty nine and 7 hundred sixty four thousandths

MOST IMPORTANT MATH KEY POINTS

Divisibility Rules

2: A number is divisible by 2 when the last digit is even.

3: A number is divisible by 3 when the sum of the digits is divisible by 3.

4: A number is divisible by 4 when the last two digits of the number are divisible by 4.

5: A number is divisible by 5 when the last digit of a number is 0 or 5.

6: A number is divisible by 6 when the number is divisible by both 2 and 3.

8: A number is divisible by 8 when the last 3 digits form a number that is divisible by 8.

9: A number is divisible by 9 when the sum of the digits of the number is divisible by 9.

10: A number is divisible by 10 when the number ends in 0.

Factors: A factor is a number that will divide into another number without a remainder.

Prime Factorization: The form of a number written as the product of its prime factors.

Example: The prime factorization of 96:

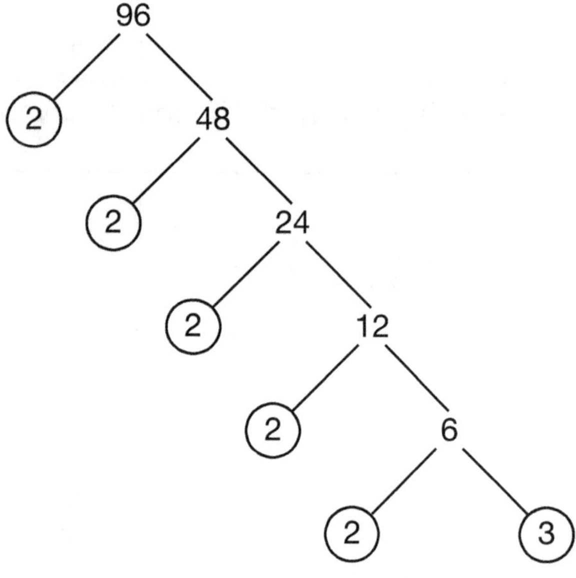

The prime factorization of 96 is $2 \cdot 2 \cdot 2 \cdot 2 \cdot 2 \cdot 3 = 2^5 \cdot 3$

One-Step Equations

One-step equations require a single operation to solve for the variable.

General Form: ax = bor x + a = b, where a and b are known numbers.

For Addition:

Equation: x+a= b
• **To Solve:** Subtract a from both sides.
•**Formula:** x = ba

Example: Solve x + 3 = 10.

Solution: Subtract 3 from both sides to isolate x.

x = 10-3=7

For Multiplication:

• **Equation:** ax = b
• **To Solve:** Divide both sides by a.
• **Formula:** $x = \dfrac{b}{a}$

Example: Solve 5x = 20.

Solution:
Divide both sides by 5 to isolate x.
$x = \dfrac{20}{5} = 4$

Two-Step Equations

Two-step equations require two operations to solve for the variable.

General Form: ax + b = c, where a, b, and c are known numbers.

Steps to Solve:
1. Isolate the variable term on one side (either by adding/subtracting).
2. Solve for the variable (either by multiplying/dividing).

Example: Solve 2x + 3 = 11.

Solution:

1. First Step: Subtract 3 from both sides to get rid of the constant term on the variable's side.
2x + 3-3 = 11-3
2x = 8
2. Second Step: Divide by 2 to isolate x.
$x = \dfrac{8}{2} = 4$

MOST IMPORTANT MATH KEY POINTS

Inequality

Inequality Symbols	Number Line Symbols
$\leq$	$\longleftarrow\!\bullet$
$\geq$	$\bullet\!\longrightarrow$
$<$	$\longleftarrow\!\circ$
$>$	$\circ\!\longrightarrow$

Study Tips

1. If $a < x$ and $x < b$, then $a < x < b$

2. If $a \leq b$, then $a < b$ or $a = b$

3. If $a \geq b$, then $a > b$ or $a = b$

4. If $a < b$ and $c < d$, then $a + c < b + d$

5. If $\dfrac{1}{a} < \dfrac{1}{x} < \dfrac{1}{b}$, then $a > x > b$ (a, x and b are positive integers)

MOST IMPORTANT MATH KEY POINTS

Unit Rate

Distance = rate x time

D = r x t

Distance = mile / miles

Rate: miles per hour (mph)

Time: hour / hours

Coordinate Plane

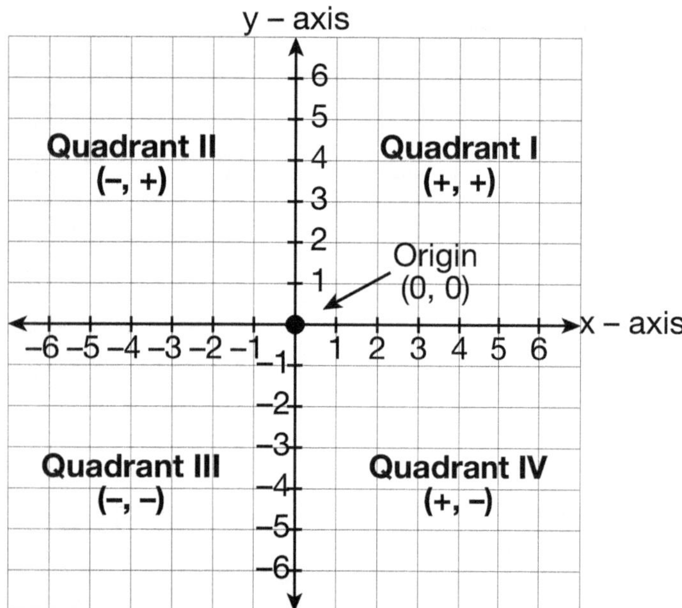

Distance Formula

$$d = \sqrt{(x_2 - x_1)^2 + (y_2 - y_1)^2}$$

Midpoint Formula

$$M = \left(\frac{x_2 + x_1}{2} , \frac{y_2 + y_1}{2} \right)$$

Ratio and Proportions

Ratio: A ratio is a comparison or relation between two quantities

Note: The ratio of a and b is written as a to b, or $\dfrac{a}{b}$

Example: Find the ratio of 35 to 45 $= \dfrac{35}{45} = \dfrac{35}{45} \div \dfrac{5}{5} = \dfrac{7}{9}$ or 7 to 9

Proportions: A proportion is an equation that shows two equivalent ratios. If $\dfrac{a}{b} = \dfrac{c}{d}$, then, by cross multiplication, ad = bc

Slope Intercept Form:

y = mx + b   m : slope

b : y – intercept = (0, b)

2-Point Slope

Suppose there are two points on a line, (x_1, y_1) and (x_2, y_2).

The slope m of the line is:

$$m = \dfrac{\text{change in y } (\text{Rise})}{\text{change in x } (\text{Run})} = \dfrac{y_2 - y_1}{x_2 - x_1}$$

MOST IMPORTANT MATH KEY POINTS

Example:

Given two points A(−2, 1) and B(4, 13), find the slope of the line passing through these points and then determine the equation of the line in slope-intercept form.

Step 1: Calculate the Slope (Two-Point Slope Formula)

The slope m of a line passing through two points (x_1, y_1) and (x_2, y_2) is given by:

$$m = \frac{y2 - y1}{x2 - x1}$$

Substituting the given points A(−2, 1) and B(4, 13) into the formula:

$$m = \frac{13 - 1}{4 - (-2)} = \frac{12}{6} = 2$$

Step 2: Find the Slope-Intercept Form $(y = mx + b)$

To find the slope-intercept form, we need the slope m and the y-intercept b. We already found m = 2. We can use either point to solve for b; let's use point A(−2, 1).

$$y = mx + b$$
$$Substitute\ m = 2,\ x = -2,\ and\ y = 1:$$
$$1 = 2(-2) + b$$
$$1 = -4 + b$$
$$b = 1 + 4$$
$$b = 5$$

Slope-Intercept Form:

Now that we have m = 2 and b = 5, the equation of the line in slope-intercept form is: y = 2x+5

Foil Method:

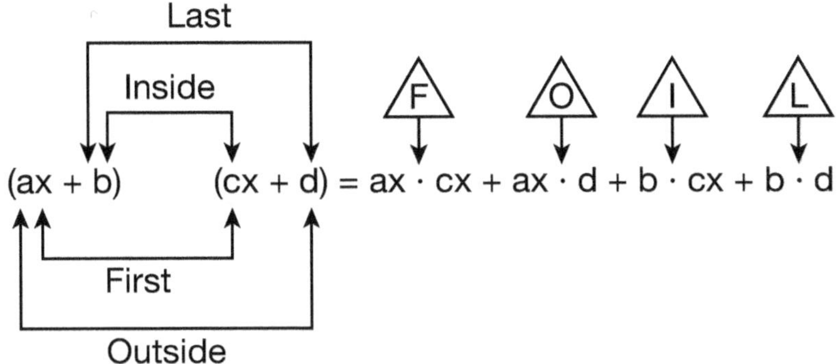

Example:

Multiply the binomials (3x + 2)(x − 5) using the FOIL method.

Solution:

- **First:** Multiply the first terms in each binomial: 3x • x = 3x².
- **Outer:** Multiply the outer terms in the binomials: 3x • (−5) = - 15x
- **Inner:** Multiply the inner terms in the binomials: 2 • x= 2x
- **Last:** Multiply the last terms in each binomial: 2 • (-5) = -10.

Now, combine these results:

(3x+2)(x-5)= 3x² - 15x + 2x - 10

Simplify by combining like terms:
3x² - 13x - 10

Thus, the product of (3x+2)(x-5) using the FOIL method is 3x² - 13x − 10.

Complex Fraction

$$\frac{\dfrac{a}{b}}{\dfrac{c}{d}} = \frac{a}{b} \cdot \frac{d}{c} = \frac{ad}{bc}$$

Example:

Simplify the complex fraction $\dfrac{\dfrac{3}{4}+\dfrac{2}{3}}{\dfrac{1}{2}-\dfrac{1}{3}}$

Solution:

Step 1: Find the LCD

First, identify the LCD of all denominators present in the complex fraction. The denominators are 4, 3, 2, and 3. The LCD of these numbers is 12.

Step 2: Multiply by the LCD

Multiply both the numerator and the denominator of the complex fraction by 1 in the form of $\dfrac{LCD}{LCD}$ to eliminate the smaller fractions. In this case, multiply both the numerator and the denominator $\dfrac{12}{12}$.

Step 3: Simplify Each Part

- **Numerator:** $\dfrac{12}{12} \cdot \left(\dfrac{3}{4}+\dfrac{2}{3}\right) = \dfrac{12 \cdot \frac{3}{4} + 12 \cdot \frac{2}{3}}{12} = \dfrac{9+8}{12} = \dfrac{17}{12}$

- **Denominator:** $\dfrac{12}{12} \cdot \left(\dfrac{1}{2}-\dfrac{1}{3}\right) = \dfrac{12 \cdot \frac{1}{2} - 12 \cdot \frac{1}{3}}{12} = \dfrac{6-4}{12} = \dfrac{2}{12} = \dfrac{1}{6}$

Step 4: Simplify the Complex Fraction

Now, simplify the complex fraction by dividing the simplified numerator by the simplified denominator:

$$\frac{\dfrac{17}{12}}{\dfrac{1}{6}} = \frac{17}{12} \cdot \frac{6}{1} = \frac{17}{2}$$

Quadratic Formula

Formula: $x = \dfrac{-b \pm \sqrt{b^2 - 4ac}}{2a}$ **for the equation** $ax^2 + c = 0.$

Example: Solve $x^2 - 4x - 5 = 0.$

Solution: Using the quadratic formula, $a = 1, b = -4, c = -5,$

$$x = \frac{4 \pm \sqrt{(-4)^2 - 4 \times 1 \times (-5)}}{2 \times 1} = \frac{4 \pm \sqrt{16 + 20}}{2} = \frac{4 \pm \sqrt{36}}{2} = -1 \text{ or } 5.$$

Mean (Average): The sum of the numbers divided by how many numbers there are.

Example: Find the mean of 3, 5, 6, 7, 9

Solution:

Mean = $\dfrac{\text{Sum of the numbers}}{\text{How many numbers}}$

Mean = $\dfrac{3 + 5 + 6 + 7 + 9}{\text{How many numbers}}$ = 30/5 = 6

Median: The middle number.
- Put all of the numbers from smallest to largest
- The median is the middle number.
- If there is an even amount of numbers, the median is the average of the two middle numbers.

Example: Find the median of 3, 12, 20, 8, 16, 30.
- Solution: Put all of the numbers into order: 3, 8, 12, 16, 20, 30. The middle numbers are

12 and 16. The average of these two number are $\dfrac{12 + 16}{2} = 14$

Mode: The most frequent value.

Example: Find the mode: A, B, C, D, C, A, B, A, C, D, C

Solution: The most repeated letter is C

Range: The difference between the lowest and highest value.

MOST IMPORTANT MATH KEY POINTS

Example: Find the range of 2, 4, 20, 30, 50, 80.

Solution: Range = 80 -2 = 78

Sum of the First n Natural Numbers

Formula: $S_n = \dfrac{n(n+1)}{2}$

Example: Find the sum of the first 5 natural numbers.

Solution: Using the formula with n = 5,

$$S_5 = \dfrac{5(5+1)}{2} = \dfrac{5 \times 6}{2} = 15$$

Sum of the First n Odd Numbers

Formula: $S_{odd} = n^2$

Example: Find the sum of the first 4 odd numbers.

Solution: Using the formula with n = 4,

$$S_{odd} = 4^2 = 16$$

Sum of the First n Even Numbers

Formula: $S_{even} = n(n + 1)$

Example: Find the sum of the first 4 even numbers.

Solution: Using the formula with n = 4,

$$S_{even} = 4(4 + 1) = 4 \times 5 = 20$$

Sum of an Arithmetic Series

Formula: $S_n = \dfrac{n}{2}(a_1 + a_n)$

Example: Find the sum of the first 5 terms of the arithmetic series 2, 4, 6, 8, 10.

Solution: Using the formula with n = 5, a_1 = 2 and a_5 = 2,

$$S_5 = \dfrac{5}{2}(2+10) = \dfrac{5}{2} \times 12 = 30$$

Sum of a Geometric Series

Formula: $S_n = \dfrac{a(1-r^n)}{1-r}$ for finite series.

Example: Find the sum of the first 3 terms of the geometric series 3, 9, 27.

Solution: Using the formula with a = 3, r = 3, and n = 3,

$$S_3 = \frac{3(1-3^3)}{1-3} = \frac{3(1-27)}{-2} = \frac{-78}{-2} = 39$$

Sum of the Squares of the First n Natural Numbers

Formula: $S_{n^2} = \dfrac{n(n+1)(2n+1)}{6}$

Example: Find the sum of the squares of the first 3 natural numbers.

Solution: Using the formula with n = 3,

$$S_{3^2} = \frac{3(3+1)(2\times3+1)}{6} = \frac{3\times4\times7}{6} = 14$$

MOST IMPORTANT MATH KEY POINTS

Least Common Multiple (LCM): The least common multiple of two numbers is the smallest integer that is a multiple of both numbers.

Example: Find the LCM of 15 and 20.

Solution:

Multiples of 15: 0, 15, 30, 45, 60, …

Multiples of 20: 0, 20, 40, 60, …

60 is the least common multiple of 15 and 20.

Greatest Common Factor (GCF): The largest number that is a factor of two or more numbers.

Example: Find the GCF of 10 and 15.

Factors of 10:1, 2, **5**, 10

Factors of 15: 1, 3, **5**, 15

So, 5 is the greatest common factor of 10 and 15.

Absolute Value: The distance of integers from zero on the number line.

$$\text{If } |x| < a \longrightarrow -a < x < a$$

$$\text{If } |x| \leq a \longrightarrow -a \leq x \leq a$$

Examples:

$|x| < 3$, then $-3 < x < 3$

$|x| \leq 7$, then $-7 \leq x \leq 7$

If $|ax + b| = c$, then $ax + b = \mp c$

Example:

If $|2x + 3| = 9$, then $2x + 3 = \mp 9$,

$2x + 3 = 9$ or $2x + 3 = -9$, $2x = 6$, $x = 3$ or $2x = -12$, $x = -6$

Fractions: Fractions are numbers that can be in the form A/B where B is not equal to zero.

Factoring

✓ $(a + b)^2 = a^2 + 2ab + b^2$

Example:

$(x + 3)^2 = x^2 + 6x + 9$

✓ $(a - b)^2 = a^2 - 2ab + b^2$

Example:

$(x - 4)^2 = x^2 - 8x + 16$

✓ $a^2 - b^2 = (a - b)(a + b)$

Example:

$(4x^2 - 9y^2 = (2x - 3y)(2x + 3y)$

✓ $a^3 - b^3 = (a - b)(a^2 + 2ab + b^2)$

Example:

$8x^3 - 27y^3 = (2x - 3y)(4x^2 + 12xy + 9y^2)$

Summative Formulas

✓ $1 + 2 + 3 + 4 + 5 + 6 + 7 + \cdots \ldots\ldots\ldots\ldots k = \dfrac{k(k + 1)}{2}$

✓ $2 + 4 + 6 + 8 + 10 + 12 + 14 + \cdots \ldots\ldots\ldots\ldots 2k = k(k + 1)$

Example: Find $1 + 2 + 3 + 4 + 5 + 6 + 8 + 9 + \ldots + 24 = ?$

Distance, Speed, and Time

Formula: Distance = Speed × Time

Example: If a car travels at a speed of 60 km/h for 2 hours, how far does it go?
Solution: Distance = 60 km/h x 2 h = 120 km

Simple Interest

Formula: $I = P \times r \times t$

Where I is the interest, P is the principal amount, r is the rate of interest per year, and t is the time in years.

Example: What is the interest on a loan of $1,000 at an annual interest rate of 5% for 3 years?

Solution: Interest = 1000* 0.05*3= $150

Permutations

Formula: P(n,r) = $\dfrac{n!}{(n-r)!}$

Example: How many ways can 4 different books be arranged on a shelf if you have 6 books to choose from?

Solution: Using the permutation formula, P(6, 4) = $\dfrac{6!}{(6-4)!}$ = $\dfrac{6!}{2!}$ = 360 ways

Combinations

Formula: $C(n,r) = \dfrac{n!}{r!\,(n-r)!}$

Example: How many ways can you choose 3 books from a set of 5?

Solution: Using the combination formula, $C(5, 3) = \dfrac{5!}{3!\,2!} = 10$ ways.

Factorial

Formula: n! = n × (n − 1) × ... × 2 × 1

Example: Calculate 5!.

Solution: 5!= 5 × 4 × 3 × 2 × 1 = 120.

Diagonal of a Polygon

Formula: $D = \dfrac{n\,(n-3)}{2}$, where n is the number of sides.

Example: How many diagonals does a hexagon have?

Solution: $D = \dfrac{6\,(6-3)}{2} = 9$ diagonals.

Sum of Angles in a Polygon

Formula: S = (n − 2) × 180°, where n is the number of sides.

Example: Find the sum of the interior angles of a pentagon.

Solution: S = (5 −2) × 180° = 3 × 180° = 540°.

Laws of Exponents		Example
Product of Powers	$a^x \times a^y = a^{x+y}$	$5^3 \times 5^6 = 5^{3+6} = 5^9$
Quotient of Powers	$a^x \div a^y = a^{x-y}$	$7^4 \div 7^3 = 7^{4-3} = 7^1$
Power of a Power	$(a^x)^y = a^{xy}$	$(3^2)^5 = 3^{2 \times 5} = 3^{10}$
Power of a Quotient	$(ab)^x = a^x b^y$	$(2x)^6 = 2^{6 \times 6} = 6^{4 \times 6}$
Power of a Fraction	$\left(\dfrac{a}{b}\right)^x = \dfrac{a^x}{b^y}$	$\left(\dfrac{2}{3}\right)^5 = \dfrac{2^5}{3^5} = \dfrac{32}{243}$
Zero Exponent	$a^0 = 1$	$(345)^0 = 1$
Negative Exponent	$a^{-x} = \dfrac{1}{a^x}$	$3^{-1} = \dfrac{1}{3}$
Fractional Exponent	$a^{\frac{x}{y}} = \sqrt[y]{a^x}$	$2^{\frac{1}{3}} = \sqrt[3]{2^1} = \sqrt[3]{2}$

Addition of Integers

Positive + Positive Positive: 5+ 3 = 8

Negative + Negative = Negative: (-5) + (−3) = −8

• Positive + Negative (or Negative + Positive): Subtract the smaller absolute value from the larger absolute value. The result takes the sign of the number with the larger absolute value.

    • Example: 5+ (-3) = 2 and (-5) + 3 = -2

Subtraction of Integers (Think of subtraction as adding the opposite.)

Subtracting a Positive: 5 - 3 = 2

• Subtracting a Negative (adding a positive): (−5) − (−3) = −5 + 3 = −2

• To subtract, add the additive inverse (opposite) of the second number: a - b = a + (−b)

    •Example: 3-(-2)=3+2=5

Multiplication of Integers

• Positive x Positive Positive: 5 x 3 = 15

• Negative × Negative = Positive: (-5) × (−3) = 15

• Positive Negative = Negative (and vice versa): 5 × (−3) = -15 and (-5) × 3 = -15

Division of Integers

• Positive ÷ Positive = Positive: 15 ÷ 3 = 5

• Negative ÷ Negative = Positive: (-15) ÷) (-3) = 5

• Positive ÷Negative = Negative (and vice versa): 15 ÷ (−3) = −5 and (-15) ÷ 3 = -5

PROBABILITY

Probability: Probabillity is a fraction or decimal comparing the number of favorable (desired) outcomes to the total number of possible outcomes. It is a number between and includes the numbers 0 and 1.

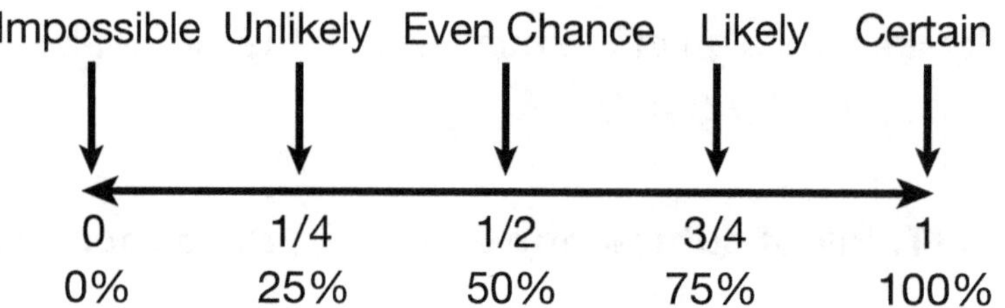

$$\textbf{Probability} = \frac{\text{Number of Desired Outcomes}}{\text{Total Number Of Possible Outcomes}}$$

Example: A letter is chosen at random from the word Mathematics. What is the probability of choosing a?

$$\textbf{Probability} = \frac{\text{Number of Desired Outcomes}}{\text{Total Number Of Possible Outcomes}}$$

$$P = \frac{2}{11}$$

Parallelogram	Area = base x height $P = 2(a + b)$	
Triangle	Area = $\dfrac{\text{base x height}}{2}$ $P = a + b + c$	
Rectangle	Area = base x height $P = 2(h + b)$	
Equilateral triangle	Area = $\dfrac{\sqrt{3}}{4}$ x a^2 $P = 3a$	
Square	Area = width x length $P = 4s$	
Trapezoid	Area = $\dfrac{(b_1 + b_2)}{2}$ x h $P = m + n + b_1 + b_2$	

Segment: A region of a circle which is "cut off" from the rest of the circle by a secant or a chord.

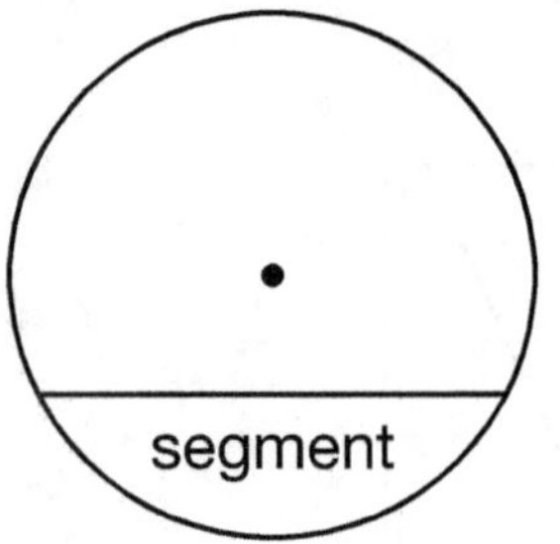

Area of a Circle:

$A = \pi r^2$

Circumference:

$C = 2\pi r$

Semi–Circle:

$A = \dfrac{1}{2}\pi r^2$

Pythagorean theorem:

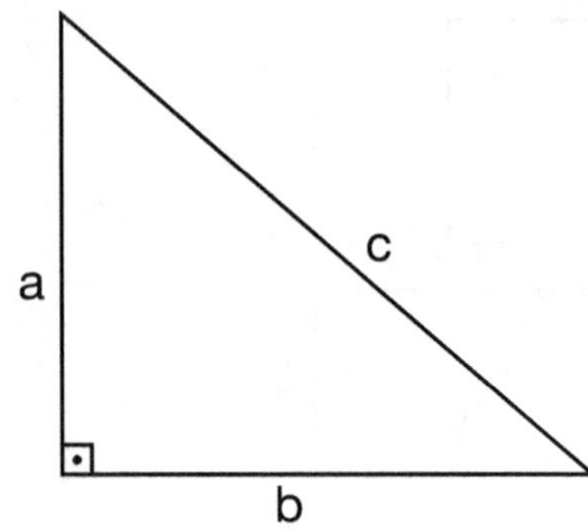

$a^2 + b^2 = c^2$

VOLUME

Right rectangular prism

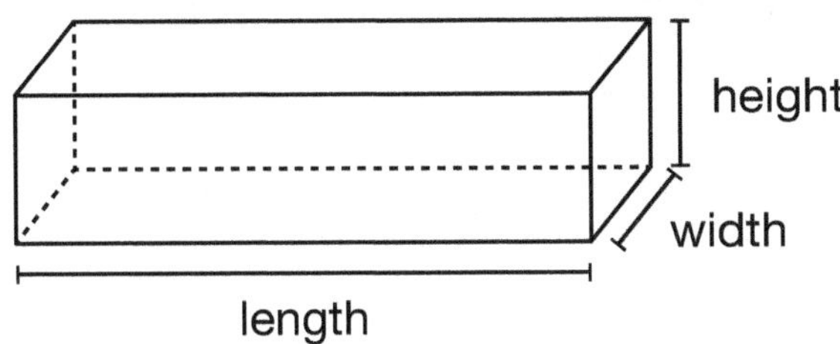

$$V = l \times w \times h$$

Cube

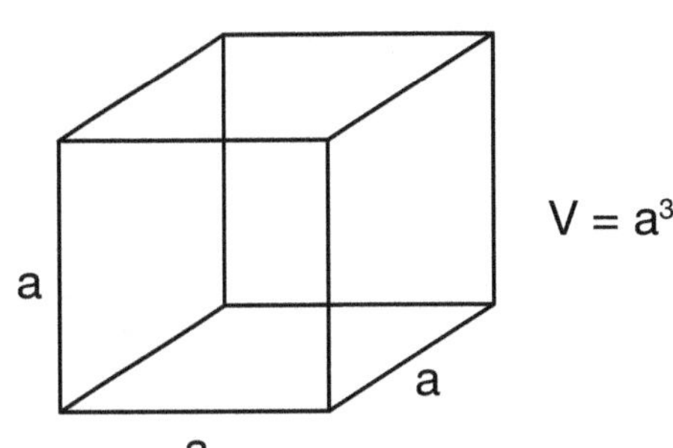

$$V = a^3$$

Cylinder

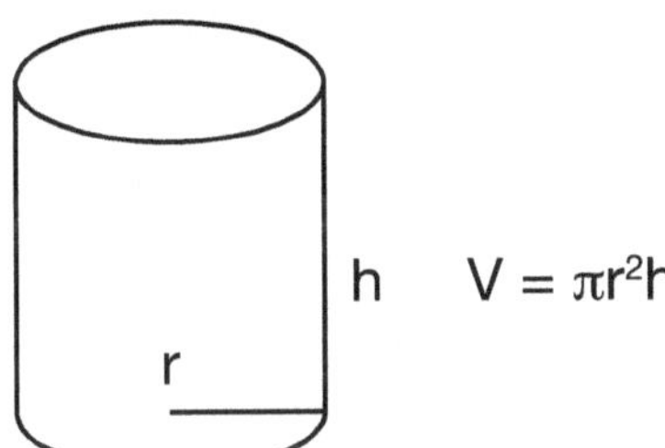

$$V = \pi r^2 h$$

Cone

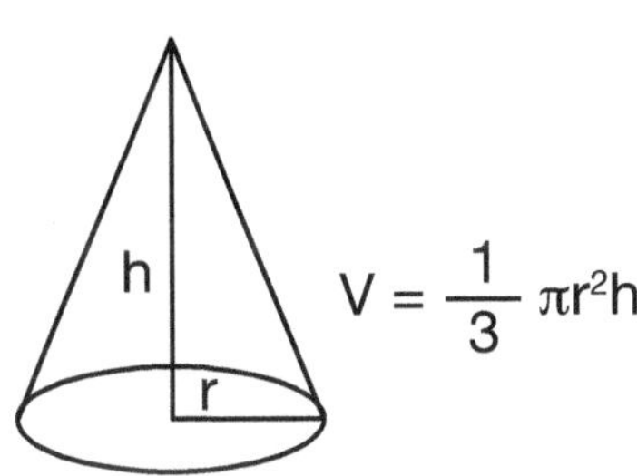

$$V = \frac{1}{3}\pi r^2 h$$

Pyramid

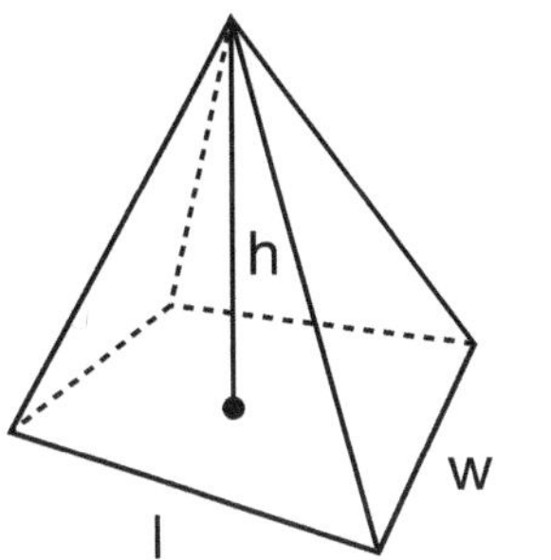

$$V = \frac{1}{3}(l \cdot w \cdot h)$$

Sphere

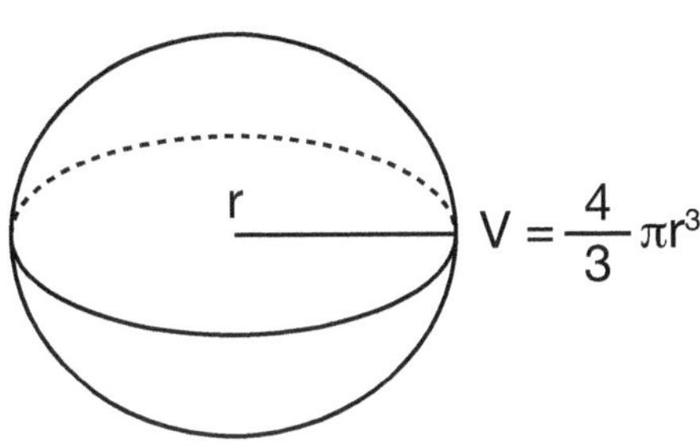

$$V = \frac{4}{3}\pi r^3$$

1) Find the 4th power of the second prime number.

A) 16 B) 81 C) 256 D) 27

2)

$$\begin{array}{r} 6\ 1\ z \\ 4\ z\ z \\ +\ z\ z\ z \\ \hline 1\ z\ 5\ 6 \end{array}$$

In the addition problem above, the letters z represent a single digit. What is the value of 3z?

A) 5 B) 6 C) 8 D) 12

3) If the exterior angle of a regular polygon is 30 degrees. How many sides does it have?

A) 12 B) 10 C) 8 D) 6

4) How many prime numbers are there between 1 and 10?

    A) 4   B) 5   C) 6   D) 3

5) If $x + y = 10$ and $x - y = 2$, what is x?

    A) 4   B) 5   C) 6   D) 7

6) What is the greatest common divisor (GCD) of 48 and 64?

    A) 16   B) 32   C) 48   D) 12

7) If $a : b = 2:3$ and $b : c = 4: 5$, what is $a : c$?

A) 8:15   B) 2:5   C) 6:10   D) 1:2

8) If $5^x = 125$, what is x?

A) 2   B) 3   C) 4   D) 5

9) If the area of a square is 64 sq units, what is the length of one side?

A) 2   B) 4   C) 6   D) 8

10) What is the product of the prime numbers between 1 and 6?

A) 5   B) 10   C) 15   D) 30

11) If the perimeter of a square is 24 units, what is the length of one side?

A) 4 units   B) 6 units   C) 8 units   D) 12 units

12) A triangle has angles measuring 45 degrees and 90 degrees. What is the measure of the third angle?

A) 45 degrees   B) 55 degrees   C) 90 degrees   D) 135 degrees

1) Calculate the sum of the following numbers:
427 +389 + 561 +678 + 832

A) 2787   B) 2887   C) 2987   D) 3087

2) The first 50 even counting numbers are written down. How many times does the digit '4' appear?

A) 14   B) 15   C) 20   D) 19

3) Maria has a piece of paper shaped like a rectangle that measures 10 cm by 14 cm. She folds it in half twice, first horizontally and then vertically. The new rectangle looks just like the original rectangle but smaller. What is the area of the new smaller rectangle in square cm?

A) 35 cm2   B) 70 cm2   C) 140 cm2   D) 175 cm2

4) In the following cryptarithmetic problem, each different letter represents a different digit in the 5-digit numbers. If C ≠ 0, what is the smallest sum possible?

```
  CLOUD
  CLOUT
+ COULD
-------
```

A)32773 B)52230 C)51120 D)50010

5) Reduce the complex fraction to a common fraction in lowest terms:

$$\frac{\frac{3}{5}}{2+\frac{1}{1+\frac{1}{4}}}$$

A) 3/14 B) 3/16 C) 3/18 D) 3/20

6) The two tokens with the question mark have the same number. The sum of the four tokens shown is 24. What is the value of one of the missing numbers?

$5+?+? +3=24$

A) 7 B) 8 C) 9 D) 10

7) A sequence of numbers follows a specific pattern: 2, 6, 12, 20, 30, ...
What is the next number in the sequence?

A) 42   B) 40   C) 38   D) 36

8) Four friends - Alex, Bella, Carlos, and Diana – are suspects in a case where a piece of artwork was accidentally damaged during their art class. The teacher asked each of them who damaged the artwork, and they gave the following statements:

- Alex: "Diana did it."
- Bella: "I did not do it."
- Carlos: "It was not me."
- Diana: "Bella is lying."

It is known that only one of them is telling the truth. Who damaged the artwork?

A) Alex   B) Bella   C) Carlos   D) Diana

9) Solve the following two-step equation for x:
$3(2x-4)= 18$

A) 2   B) 4   C) 5   D) 6

10) Lucas collects stamps, and each year for his birthday he receives stamps from his family. For his first birthday, he received 5 stamps. For his second birthday, he received 10 stamps. For each subsequent birthday, he received 5 more stamps than the previous year. How many stamps does Lucas have in total if he is 7 years old?

A) 105 stamps   B) 140 stamps   C) 175 stamps   D) 210 stamps

11) Sara has three times as many stickers as Mike. If Mike has 12 stickers, how many stickers do they have in total?

A) 48   B) 36   C) 24   D) 60

12) A rectangle's length is twice its width. If the perimeter of the rectangle is 36 cm, what is the area of the rectangle?

A) 32 cm^2 B) 48 cm^2 C) 64 cm^2 D) 72 cm^2

1) What is the sum of $\frac{8}{3}$ and $\frac{5}{4}$?

A) $3\frac{1}{3}$
B) $3\frac{2}{3}$
C) $3\frac{11}{12}$
D) $4\frac{1}{12}$

2) What is 50% in reduced fraction form?

A) $\frac{1}{2}$
B) $\frac{2}{4}$
C) $\frac{50}{100}$
D) $\frac{25}{50}$

3) While on a journey, you decide to note the speed of your vehicle. For 3 hours, the vehicle maintains a speed of 70 mph. For the next 1 hour and 45 minutes, the speed is reduced to 50 mph, and for the final 2 hours, the speed is increased to 75 mph. What percentage of the journey is the vehicle traveling at or above 70 mph? (Round to the nearest tenth of a percent.)

A) 62.5%
B) 74.1 %
C) 83.3%
D) 55.6%

4) If Lisa sets aside 20% of her monthly income for a vacation fund, and her monthly income is $2,000, how much will she have saved after 6 months?

A) $2,400   B) $1,200   C) $2,000   D) $1,800

5) Tom wants to purchase a new video game that costs $60. He decides to save $10 in the first week and increases his savings by $2 each subsequent week ($12 in the second week, $14 in the third week, and so on). How many weeks will it take for Tom to save enough money to buy the video game?

A) 5 weeks   B) 6 weeks   C) 7 weeks   D) 8 weeks

6) Linda planted a flower in her garden that grows 3 inches taller each month. Initially, when the flower was planted, it was 5 inches tall. If the pattern of growth continues, how many months will it take for the flower to reach 20 inches tall?

A) 4 months   B) 5 months   C) 6 months   D) 7 months

7) Write 40% in reduced fraction form.

A) $\frac{40}{100}$ B) $\frac{2}{5}$ C) $\frac{4}{10}$ D) $\frac{8}{20}$

8) On the first day of training, Sarah runs 2 miles. On the second day, she increases her distance by 1 mile, running 3 miles, and continues to add 1 mile to her distance each day. How many miles will Sarah run on the fifth day?

A) 5 miles B) 6 miles C) 7 miles D) 8 miles

9) If a bicycle costs half of your total savings, and you find it on discount for $\frac{3}{4}$ of its listed price, what fraction of your savings did you ultimately spend on the bicycle?

A) $\frac{3}{8}$ B) $\frac{1}{2}$ C) $\frac{2}{5}$ D) $\frac{3}{7}$

10) Compute the prime factorization of 180.

A) 2×9×10   B) 2×2×3×3×5   C) 4×45   D) 6×30

11) What is 3487.521 rounded to the nearest 100?

A) 3400   B) 3500   C) 3480   D) 3490

12) Mike wants to purchase a new video game console that costs $300.00, but he has saved only one- third of that cost. How much more money does Mike need to save before he has enough to buy the video game console?

A) $100.00   B) $200.00   C) $250.00   D) $150.00

1) Evaluate the expression $\frac{123}{1+1+1}$.

A) 41   B) 123   C) 36   D) 45

2) How many inches shorter is 3.5 feet than 5.5 feet?

A) 24 inches   B) 20 inches   C) 18 inches   D) 14 inches

3) The Rosewood Theatre sells tickets at a price of $10 for adults and $6 for children. If they make $660 from a show with an audience of 80 people, how many children bought tickets?

A) 30   B) 35   C) 40   D) 45

4) Emma's favorite number has a remainder of 2 when divided by 3, and a remainder of 3 when divided by 7. If Emma's favorite number is positive, what is the smallest possible value of her favorite number?

A) 17   B) 23   C) 31   D) 41

5) Lila and Maya both draw squares. No matter how large Lila draws her square, Maya's square will always have 4 times the area. If Lila's square has a side length of 5 cm, how long will one side of Maya's square be in centimeters?

A) 10 cm   B) 20 cm   C) 5 cm   D) 40 cm

6) Alice has a drawer containing 8 pairs of socks, with each pair being a different color. If she randomly selects socks from the drawer, how many socks must she pick to ensure she has at least one matching pair?

A) 8   B) 9   C) 16   D) 17

7) Sarah currently has 40 marbles, while her younger sister Emma has 20 marbles. Sarah decides to give some of her marbles to Emma so that they both have an equal number of marbles. How many marbles will Sarah give to Emma?

A) 5   B) 10   C) 15   D) 20

8) Five years ago, John was three times as old as Anna. If John is currently 20 years old, how old is Anna now?

A) 5   B) 10   C) 15   D) 25

9) In a bag of fruit, the ratio of apples to oranges is 2:3. If there are 15 oranges in the bag, how many apples are there?

A) 5   B) 10   C) 15   D) 20

10) Solve for x in the equation: $3(x + 2) - 4 = 14$

A) $x = 4$ B) $x = 5$ C) $x = 6$ D) $x = 7$

11) Solve for x in the equation: $2x - 5 = 3(x + 1)$.

A) $x = -4$ B) $x = -8$ C) $x = -10$ D) $x = -12$

12) What is the prime factorization of 360?

A) $2^3 \times 3^2 \times 5$ B) $2^3 \times 3^2 \times 5^2$ C) $2^4 \times 3^2 \times 5$ D) $2^4 \times 3^3 \times 5$

1) Find the value of 92-81+73-62 +58-47+36-25.

A) 44   B) 46   C) 48   D) 50

2) Emma selects five different numbers from the list 1, 2, 3, 4, 5, 6, 7, 8, 9, 11. Among her chosen numbers are 6 and 7, which are the only consecutive numbers she picks. What is the maximum possible sum of the five numbers Emma chooses?

A) 30   B) 37   C) 42   D) 43

3) Mia uses the digits 1, 2, 3, 7, 8, and 9 to create two 3-digit numbers. Each digit is used exactly once. The two numbers are then subtracted from one another. What is the maximum possible difference between the two numbers?

A) 666   B) 864   C) 876   D) 896

4) How many 3-digit numbers are multiples of 14?

A) 64   B) 63   C) 60   D) 59

5) What is the 4th power of the second prime number?

A) 27   B) 81   C) 64   D) 256

6)
$$
\begin{array}{r}
6\,a\,b \\
4\,b\,a \\
+\,a\,a\,b \\
\hline
1\,3\,b\,0
\end{array}
$$
Find $a + b = ?$

A) 3   B) 6   C) 7   D) 8

7) How many diagonals does a hexagon have?

A) 6 B) 9 C) 12 D) 15

8) Simplify the expression: $4(x+6)-5(2x-3)+2x=?$

A) $-4x + 39$ B) $-4x-39$ C) $4x + 39$ D) $4x - 39$

9) If $\frac{3}{2}(2x+4)= 6$, then solve for x?

A) 0 B) 1 C) -1 D) 2

10) Liam has two whole numbers. Their product is 36 and their sum is 13. What is the smaller number?

A) 3   B) 4   C) 6   D) 9

11) The length of polygon ABCDEF has AB=9, BC=10, FA=6 and FE=5. What is DE + DC?

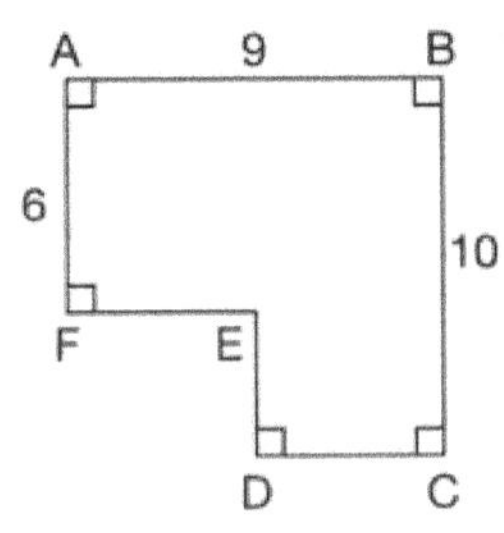

A) 6   B) 8   C) 12   D) 16

12) A recipe for lemonade requires 3 cups of water for every 1 cup of lemon juice. If you have 12 cups of water, how many cups of lemon juice do you need to make the lemonade?

A) 3 cups   B) 4 cups   C) 6 cups   D) 9 cups

1) What fraction represents half of a quarter?

A) $\frac{1}{4}$ B) $\frac{1}{2}$ C) $\frac{1}{8}$ D) $\frac{2}{4}$

2) A bag contains red, blue, and green marbles only. If there are 3 red marbles, 2 blue marbles, and 5 green marbles, what is the probability of picking a green marble?

A) $\frac{1}{2}$ B) $\frac{5}{10}$ C) $\frac{5}{2}$ D) $\frac{2}{4}$

3) A sequence starts with 1 and the next number is obtained by adding 5 and then dividing by 2. What is the third number in the sequence?

A) 3   B) 4   C) 5   D) 6

4) If the sum of three consecutive even numbers is 54, what is the smallest of these numbers?

A) 16 B) 18 C) 20 D) 22

5) What is the smallest two-digit number that, when reversed, results in a number that is 9 less than the original number?

A) 12 B) 21 C) 31 D) 41

6) In a class of 40 students, 25% wear glasses. How many students do not wear glasses?

A) 10 B) 30 C) 20 D) 15

7) If you flip a coin three times, what is the probability of getting heads at least once?

A) $\frac{1}{2}$ B) $\frac{3}{4}$ C) $\frac{7}{8}$ D) $\frac{1}{8}$

8) A number consists of two digits whose sum is 13. If the digits are reversed, the new number is 27 more than the original number. What is the original number?

A) 58 B) 76 C) 49 D) 85

9) A sequence of numbers starts with 1, 11, 21, 1211, 111221. What is the next number in the sequence?

A) 312211 B) 13112221 C) 1113213211 D) 221213

10) In the same code, where "BIRD" is written as "DRIb", how would "MOON" be translated?

A) NOOm   B) NOON   C) NOOM   D) NOON

11) Simplify the complex fraction: $\dfrac{\frac{3}{4} - \frac{1}{2}}{\frac{1}{3} + \frac{1}{6}}$.

A) $\dfrac{3}{2}$ B) $\dfrac{1}{2}$ C) $\dfrac{2}{3}$ D) $\dfrac{3}{4}$

12) Consider the following sequence: 2, 6, 12, 20, 30, ...
What is the next number in the sequence?

A) 40   B) 42   C) 45   D) 48

1) How many rectangles are there in the figure below?

A)8   B)9   C)16   D)18

2) There were 800 members in a book club last year. The number of members decreased by 12% this year. How m any members are there in the book club this year?

A) 704   B) 712   C) 720   D) 728

3) The product of two even numbers is always _______.

A) even   B) divisible by 3   C. Odd   D. greater than 2

4) The letters in the word BIOLOGY were put in a box. What is the chance of getting the letter O?

A) 1 out of 7   B) 2 out of 7   C) 1 out of 6   D) 2 out of 6

5) Ms. Lin received a shipment of books. She sold 2/5 of the books in the morning and sold 200 books in the afternoon. At the end of the day, she found that 1/3 of the books were not sold. How many books did she receive in the beginning?

A) 600   B) 750   C) 900   D) 1050

6) John saved $20 in the first month, $40 in the second month, $60 in the third month, and so forth. The amount of money he saved in the last month was $160. How much money did John save in total?

A) 480   B) 640   C) 720   D) 800

7) A number is subtracted from 10. The difference is then multiplied by 4. When 6 is added to the product, the result is 22. What is this number?

A) 6   B) 4   C) 3   D) 2

8) How many numbers are there in the sequence 4, 9, 14, ..., 99, 104?

A) 20   B) 21   C) 22   D) 25

9) Two trees are planted in Mr. Idris's orchard. One is 30 cm tall, and it grows 2 cm every 3 years. The other is 45 cm tall, and it grows 3 cm every 5 years. In how many years will the two trees be the same height?

A) 45 years   B) 60 years   C) 190 years   D) 225 years

10) I added the first eight whole numbers greater than 0. I forgot to include one whole number and I got 30 as the sum. Which one of these eight whole numbers did I not add?

A) 1 B) 2 C) 6 D) 8

11) ind the value of the series: (Round your answer to nearest hundredth)
$0.2 + 0.22 + 0.222 + ... + 0.2222222222$

A) 1.30 B) 1.65 C) 2.00 D) 3.19

12) Find the missing number in the box.

$2 \times \square \div (4 \times 3) - 2 = 50$

A) 300 B) 310 C) 312 D) 320

1) What number is 15 more than the greatest whole number less than 50?

A) 64   B) 65   C) 66   D) 67

2) What number is the sum of 40 + 40 + 40 equal to each of the following except?

A) 60 + 60   B) 50 + 70   C) 30 + 30 + 30 + 30   D) 20 + 20 + 20 + 20 + 20

3) If I have 5 more than 4 dozen cookies, how many cookies do I have?

A) 53   B) 54   C) 58   D) 60

4) What is the largest whole number less than 50 that is a multiple of 7?

A) 42   B) 45   C) 47   D) 49

5) Juan's 8th birthday will be in 2010. His 12th birthday will be in what year?

A) 2012   B) 2014   C) 2015 D   ) 2016

6) A gardener planted 2 trees on the first day. If he plants twice as many trees each day as the day before, how many trees will he plant 3 days from the first day?

A) 8   B) 12   C) 16   D) 24

7) The tens' digit of the product 5678×2345 is?

A) 1 B) 2 C) 7 D) 0

Solution:

8) Sara turned 8 years old four months ago. Sara will turn 11 years old in months.

A) 28 B) 32 C) 36 D) 40

9) What is the correct time exactly 50 minutes after 11:00 AM?

A) 11:50 AM B) 12:00 PM C) 11:40 AM D) 12:10 PM

10) The librarian is 15 years older than my sister, who is three times my age. If I am 7, how old is the librarian?"

A) 36   B) 42   C) 45   D) 51

11) To compute the square of a number, just multiply the number by itself. What is the square of 13?"

A) 100   B) 120   C) 144   D) 169

12) At the book donation event, my group donated 7 books for every 2 books your group donated. If your group donated 28 books, then my group donated ? books.

A) 49   B) 98   C) 77   D) 56

1) Determine the smallest fraction from the following group ($\frac{1}{6}$, $\frac{1}{7}$, $\frac{1}{8}$, $\frac{1}{9}$, $\frac{1}{11}$)

A) $\frac{1}{6}$ B) $\frac{1}{7}$ C) $\frac{1}{8}$ D) $\frac{1}{11}$

2) Which of the following is equal to $\frac{45}{75}$?

A) 6:10 B) 5:8 C) 9:15 D) 3:5

3) The ratio of boys to girls at Newton Public School is 5: 6. If there are 150 boys at the school, then how many students are there at the school?

A) 180 B) 300 C) 330 D) 360

4) A set of five different positive integers has a mean of 22 and a median of 22. What is the smallest possible integer in the set?

A) 18   B) 20   C) 22   D) 24

5) A test has four questions with each question worth one mark. If 10% of the students got O questions correct, 20% got 1 question correct, 30% got 2 questions correct, 25% got 3 questions correct, and 15% got all 4 questions correct, then what was the overall class mean mark?

A) 2.0   B) 2.2   C) 2.5   D) 2.8

6) Calculate the sum: $2 + 4 + 6 + ... + 98 + 100$.

A) 2550   B) 2600   C) 5050   D) 2552

7) The value of $\dfrac{1}{3-\dfrac{1}{3-\frac{1}{3}}}$ is equal to _______.

A) $\frac{1}{2}$
B) $\frac{2}{3}$
C) $\frac{3}{4}$
D) $\frac{8}{21}$

8) When you multiply Jane's age and Alex's age, you get 24. If you add their ages together, you get 10. Jane is older than Alex. How old is Alex?

A) 6
B) 4
C) 2
D) 3

9) The sum of the digits of all positive primes less than 10 is

A) 17
B) 10
C) 8
D) 4

10) Of the following, which is between $\frac{1}{4}$ and $\frac{2}{3}$?

A) 0.3   B) 0.5   C) 0.7   D) 0.9

11) If 4 out of 6 teachers recommend reading fiction, what percent do not recommend reading fiction?

A) 25%   B) 33%   C) 50%   D) 66%

12) Michael scored 85, 90, 87, 80, and 92 on his science tests. He has to take one more test. What is the lowest score Michael can earn on his last test and still achieve a mean of at least 86?

A) 80   B) 81   C) 82   D) 95

1) What is the greatest common factor of 36 and 48?

    A) 6   B) 12   C) 18   D) 24

2) If $\frac{1}{2}$ of a number is 3, what is $\frac{1}{4}$ of the same number?

    A) 1.5   B) 6   C) 12   D) 3

3) Which shape has exactly four right angles?

    A) Triangle   B) Circle   C) Rectangle   D) Trapezoid

4) Sarah has 12 apples. If she gives away 1/3 of her apples, how many does she have left?

A) 4   B) 8   C) 16   D) 9

5) If a triangle has angles of 35° and 65°, what is the measure of the third angle?

A) 80°   B) 85°   C) 90°   D) 100°

6) What is the median of the set of numbers 4, 8, 6, 10, and 2?

A) 2   B) 4   C) 6   D) 8

7) If you divide a number by 2 and subtract 5, the result is 3. What is the original number?

A) 10 B) 16 C) 18 D) 20

8) What is the result of $(3x^2 - 2x + 5) + (x^2 + x - 3)$?

A) $4x^2 - x + 2$ B) $4x^2 - 3x + 8$ C) $4x^2 + x + 2$ D) $3x^2 + x + 2$

9) What is the probability of rolling an even number on a six-sided die?

A) $\frac{1}{6}$ B) $\frac{1}{3}$ C) $\frac{1}{2}$ D) $\frac{2}{3}$

10) Convert 0.625 to a fraction.

A) $\frac{5}{8}$ 　　　 B) $\frac{5}{16}$ 　　　 C) $\frac{5}{4}$ 　　　 D) $\frac{3}{5}$

11) The ratio of boys to girls in a class is 3:4. If there are 12 boys, how many girls are there?

A) 12 　　　 B) 14 　　　 C) 16 　　　 D) 18

12) A tank can be filled by one pipe in 4 hours and by another pipe in 6 hours. How long will it take for both pipes working together to fill the tank?

A) 2.4 hours 　　　 B) 2.5 hours 　　　 C) 3.0 hours 　　　 D) 3.5 hours

1) A sequence of numbers begins with 1, 1, 2, 3, 5, 8. What is the next number in this Fibonacci sequence?

A) 10   B) 11   C) 12   D) 13

2) Two trains start from the same place and run in opposite directions. One goes west at 60 km/h and the other east at 70 km/h. How far apart are they after 2 hours?

A) 100 km   B) 200 km   C) 260 km   D) 140 km

3) If "MATH" is coded as "NZUI", which word is coded as "BQQMF"?

A) APPLE   B) ANNOY   C) ALONE   D) APART

4) A clock shows the time as 3:15. What is the angle between the hour and minute hands?

A) 7.5 degrees   B) 97.5 degrees   C) 187.5 degrees   D) 277.5 degrees

5) An encrypted message uses the following rule: each letter is replaced by the letter three positions down the alphabet. What does the coded message "KHOOR" decode to?

A) HELLO   B) GOODBYE   C) THERE   D) WHERE

6) A drawer contains 12 socks, each one of either black or white. If there are exactly 4 black socks, how many pairs of white socks are there?

A) 2   B) 3   C) 4   D) 5

7) In a family of 6 members P, Q, R, S, T, and U, there are two married couples. T is a teacher and the father of R. U is the grandfather of R and is a lawyer. Q is the bank manager and is married to P. P is not the mother of R. How is S related to U?

A) Daughter   B) Son   C) Daughter-in-law   D) Son-in-law

8) A bag contains red, blue, and green marbles. There are twice as many blue marbles as red marbles and three times as many green marbles as blue marbles. If there are 5 red marbles, how many marbles are there in total?

A) 45   B) 55   C) 60   D) 65

9) The product of two consecutive numbers is 56. What is the smaller number?

A) 6   B) 7   C) 8   D) 9

10) If the area of a square is 64 cm², what is the length of one side?

A) 6 cm   B) 7 cm   C) 8 cm   D) 9 cm

11) If $x + 3 = 10$, then what is x^2?

A) 49   B) 36   C) 25   D) 16

12) A rectangle has a length of 10 cm more than its width. If the width is 5 cm, what is the area?

A) 150 cm2   B) 100 cm2   C) 75 cm2   D) 50 cm2

1) Anna thinks of a number, multiplies it by 3, and then subtracts 7. The result is 20. What was the original number?

A) 9   B) 8   C) 10   D) 11

2) If five times a number minus two is 48, what is the number?

A) 10   B) 9   C) 8   D) 12

3) A farmer wants to fence a rectangular area using 300 meters of fencing. If the length is twice the width, what is the area of the rectangle?

A) 1333 sq m   B) 2000 sq m   C) 2666 sq m   D) 5000 sq m

4) What fraction is halfway between 1/4 and 3/4?

A) 1/2   B) 1/3   C) 2/5   D) 3/8

5) Find the smallest number that is divisible by both 5 and 6.

A) 10   B) 15   C) 30   D) 60

6) If you multiply a number by 3 and then subtract 7, the result is 20. What is the number?

A) 7   B) 8   C) 9   D) 10

7) What is the result when you multiply the largest single-digit number by the smallest two-digit number?

A) 81   B) 90   C) 100   D) 110

8) If you divide a number by 2 and add 5, the result is 11. What was the original number?

A) 8   B) 10   C) 12   D) 14

9) If the sum of two consecutive odd numbers is 56, what is the larger number?

A) 27   B) 29   C) 28   D) 30

10) If five times a number decreased by 2 is 48, what is the number?

A) 8 B) 9 C) 10 D) 11

11) The diagonal of a square is 10 cm. Find the area of the square.

A) 50 cm² B) 75cm² C) 100 cm² D) 125cm²

12) What is the probability of rolling an even number or a number greater than 3 on a standard six-sided die?

A) 1/3 B) 1/2 C) 2/3 D) 5/6

1) A train travels from Station A to Station B in 3 hours at a speed of 60 km/h. On the return journey, it travels at a speed of 80 km/h. How long does the return journey take?

A) 2.25 hours　　　　B) 2.5 hours　　　　C) 2.75 hours　　　　D) 3 hours

2) A rectangular field is twice as long as it is wide. If the perimeter of the field is 180 meters, what are the field's dimensions?

A) 40m by 30m　　B) 45m by 90m　　C) 40m by 80m　　D) 30m by 60m

3) If five pencils cost as much as three erasers, and one eraser costs 40 cents, how much do two pencils cost?

A) 24 cents　　B) 48 cents　　C) 60 cents　　D) 80 cents

4) Leo has some stickers. If he gives 5 stickers to each of his 4 friends, he will have 7 stickers left. How many stickers does Leo have?

A) 27   B) 28   C) 29   D) 30

5) The sum of three consecutive even numbers is 48. What is the smallest of these numbers?

A) 14   B) 12   C) 16   D) 10

6) What is the value of the expression $5^2 - (3^3 - 2^2)$?

A) 2   B) 8   C) 10   D) 16

7) 3.982 =

A. three and ninety-eight hundredths
B. thirty-nine and eighty-two hundredths
C. three and nine hundred eighty-two thousandths
D. three and ninety-two hundredths

8) What is the nearest integer to 2.49?

A) 2   B) 3   C) 2.5   D) 2.4

9) A square lawn has a side length of 40 meters. A flowerbed is planned to be built along one edge of the lawn, running the entire length of that edge, and covering 10% of the lawn's total area. What will be the width of the flowerbed?

A. 1 meter   B. 2 meters   C. 4 meters   D. 10 meters

10) Simplify the expression: $(2^4)^3 \times 2^5$.

A) 2^{17} B) 2^{20} C) 2^{23} D) 2^{32}

11) Which of the following numbers is divisible by both 4 and 9?

A) 81   B) 126   C) 144   D) 180

12) If $\frac{2}{3}$ of a cake is eaten, and then $\frac{3}{4}$ of the remaining cake is eaten, what fraction of the original cake is left?

A) $\frac{1}{3}$ B) $\frac{1}{4}$ C) $\frac{1}{6}$ D) $\frac{1}{12}$

1) A car travels at a constant speed of 60 miles per hour. How many miles will the car travel in 2.5 hours?

A) 120 miles   B) 150 miles   C) 180 miles   D) 200 miles

2) Ten years ago, Alice was twice as old as her brother. If Alice is currently 30 years old, how old is her brother?

A) 10 years   B) 15 years   C) 20 years   D) 25 years

3) Solve the following two-step equation involving fractions:

$$\frac{3}{4}x - \frac{1}{2} = \frac{5}{8}$$

A) $x = \frac{9}{16}$ B) $x = \frac{7}{8}$ C) $x = \frac{5}{16}$ D) $x = \frac{3}{2}$

4) In a certain pattern, the number of sides in each successive shape increases in the following order: Triangle, Square, Pentagon, Hexagon, ...
Based on the pattern, which shape corresponds to the 8th shape in the sequence?

A) Octagon   B) Nonagon   C) Decagon   D) Dodecagon

5) Anna is twice as old as Ben. The sum of their ages is 36 years. How old will Anna be in 4 years?

A) 20 years   B) 24 years   C) 28 years   D) 32 years

6) A car and a motorcycle set off from the same point, traveling in opposite directions. The car travels at a speed of 60 kilometers per hour, and the motorcycle at a speed of 90 kilometers per hour. How far apart will they be after 2 hours?

A) 150 kilometers   B) 180 kilometers   C) 300 kilometers   D) 320 kilometers

7) Find the missing number in the following number sequence. 2, 6, 18,_, 162, 486.

A) 54 B) 58 C) 60 D) 64

8) There are 200 pupils in a school club at first. If the number of boys increases by 10 and the number of girls decreases by 10%, the number of pupils in the club will become 194. How many boys are there in the club at first?

A) 70 B) 100 C) 110 D) 120

9) The sum of two numbers is 160. The sum of of the smaller number and 2 of the greater number is 100. Find the difference between the two numbers.

A) 20 B) 40 C) 60 D) 128

10) Of the whole numbers from 1 through 50, how many are 4 more than another whole number from 1 through 46?

A) 42 B) 46 C)48 D) 51

11) My initials are the 5th, 15th, and 19th letters of the alphabet, in that order. My name could be"

A) Edward Oscar Sullivan
B) Erin Olivia Scott
C) Emma Olive Smith
D) Ethan Oliver Sanders

12) A circumference of a circle is three times as long as a side of a square. If the circumference of the circle is 18, how long is a side of the square?

A) 2 B) 4 C) 6 D) 9

1) The area of a rectangular garden is $72\frac{1}{2}$ square meters. The length is $14\frac{1}{4}$ meters. What is the width, in meters, of the garden?

   A) 5

   B) $5\frac{1}{3}$

   C) $5\frac{5}{57}$

   D) $5\frac{3}{4}$

2) An outfit consists of a shirt, pants, and an optional jacket. If there are 5 choices of shirts, 4 choices of pants, and 2 choices of jackets (black, white), how many outfits are possible?

   A) 30

   B) 40

   C) 50

   D) 60

3) Ms. Chen's salary increases by 4 percent each year. If her salary for 2018 was $50,000, what will her salary for 2023 be?

   A) $60,832.65

   B) $61,665.12

   C) $59,270.40

   D) $58,235.53

4) If 3 is added to a number and this sum is tripled, the resultis 21. What is the number?

A) 2 B) 3 C) 4 D) 5

5) A rectangle's length is three times its width. If the perimeter is 48 cm, what is the length?

A) 9 cm B) 12 cm C) 18 cm D) 36 cm

6) If the sum of three consecutive numbers is 42, what is the smallest number?

A) 12 B) 13 C) 14 D) 15

7) In a sequence, the first term is 1 and each successive term is the sum of all previous terms plus 1. What is the fifth term in the sequence?

A) 16   B) 15   C) 31   D) 32

8) What is the smallest integer greater than 1 that is both square and a cube?

A) 8   B) 16   C) 64   D) 81

9) If the sum of the first n positive integers is 210, what is n?

A) 20   B) 21   C) 19   D) 22

10) Simplify the expression $\sqrt{50} + \sqrt{18} - \sqrt{8}$.

A) $3\sqrt{2}$ B) $5\sqrt{2}$ C) $6\sqrt{2}$ D) $9\sqrt{2}$

11) A water tank is filled by two pipes. The first pipe alone can fill the tank in 40 minutes, and the second pipe can fill it in 60 minutes. How long will it take for both pipes to fill the tank together?

A) 24 minutes   B) 25 minutes   C) 30 minutes   D) 35 minutes

12) A number consists of two digits whose sum is 9. If the digits are reversed, the new number is 27 less than the original number. What is the original number?

A) 63   B) 54   C) 45   D) 36

1) Find the 4th power of the second prime number?

A) 16   B) 81   C) 256   D) 27

Solution:

The second prime number is 3 (the first few prime numbers are 2, 3, 5, 7...). To find its 4th power, we calculate 34.

$3^4 = 3 \times 3 \times 3 \times 3 = 81$

Therefore, the correct answer is:

Correct Answer: B

2)

$$
\begin{array}{r}
6\ 1\ z \\
4\ z\ z \\
+\ z\ z\ z \\
\hline
1\ z\ 5\ 6
\end{array}
$$

In the addition problem above, the letters z represent a single digit. What is the value of 3z?

A) 5   B) 6   C) 8   D) 12

Solution:

Let's solve this problem step by step, considering each place value:

1. Units Place: z+z+z = 6
2. Tens Place: z+z+1=5 (This confirms that there is no carryover from the units column)
3. Hundreds Place: 6+4+z =10 + z (This indicates that 2z must be a 10's multiple, which can only be true if z = 0 or z = 2. Since z cannot be 0 because 3z = 6, then z must be 2.)

From the units place, considering there is no carryover, we have $3z = 6$. Dividing both sides by 3, we get $z = 2$,

Using $z=2$, we can confirm the value of $3z$ as follows:

$3z = 3 \times 2 = 6$

Correct Answer: B

3) If the exterior angle of a regular polygon is 30 degrees, How many sides does it have?

A) 12   B) 10   C) 8   D) 6

Solution:

The sum of the exterior angles of any polygon is 360 degrees.
Each exterior angle of a regular polygon is equal: $360 \div 30 = 12$. Therefore, the polygon has 12 sides.

Correct Answer: A

4) How many prime numbers are there between 1 and 10?

A) 4   B) 5   C) 6   D) 3

Solution:

List the numbers between 1 and 10: 2, 3, 4, 5, 6, 7, 8, 9, 10.
Identify the prime numbers (divisible only by 1 and themselves): 2, 3, 5, 7.
Count: There are 4 prime numbers.

Correct Answer: A

5) If $x + y = 10$ and $x - y = 2$, what is x?

A) 4   B) 5   C) 6   D) 7

Solution:

Add the two equations: $x + y + x - y = 10 + 2$.
Simplify: $2x = 12$.
Divide by 2: $x = 6$.
To find y, substitute x back into one of the original equations: $6 + y = 10$.
Solve for y: $y = 4$.

Correct Answer: C

6) What is the greatest common divisor (GCD) of 48 and 64?

A) 16   B) 32   C) 48   D) 12

Solution:

List the divisors of 48: 1, 2, 3, 4, 6, 8, 12, 16, 24, 48.
List the divisors of 64: 1, 2, 4, 8, 16, 32, 64.
Find the largest number common to both lists: 16.
Therefore, the GCD of 48 and 64 is 16.

Correct Answer: A

7) If $a : b = 2:3$ and $b : c = 4: 5$, what is $a : c$?

A) 8:15 B) 2:5 C) 6:10 D) 1:2

Solution:

To make b consistent, we can find a common multiple of the two b values. In $a : b = 2: 3$ and $b : c = 4 : 5$, the b values can be made consistent by multiplying the first ratio by 2.

Adjusted ratios: $a : b = 4 : 6$ and $b : c = 4 : 5$.
This gives a direct ratio of a to c as $a : c = 4 : 5$.
To compare a to c directly, multiply the $a : b$ ratio to match the $b : c$ ratio : $a : c = 8: 15$ (since $4 \times 2 = 8$ and $5 \times 3 = 15$).

Correct Answer: A

8) If $5^x = 125$, what is x?

A) 2 B) 3 C) 4 D) 5

Solution:
1. Recognize that 125 is a power of 5: $125 = 5^3$.
2. Therefore, $x = 3$ to satisfy $5^x = 125$.

Correct Answer: B

9) If the area of a square is 64 sq units, what is the length of one side?

A) 2   B) 4   C) 6   D) 8

Solution:

The area of a square is given by the formula: Area = $side^2$.
We have the area, 64 sq units, so set this equal to $side^2$: $side^2 = 64$.
To find the side, take the square root of both sides: side = $\sqrt{64}$.
Calculate the square root: side = 8 units.

Correct Answer: D

10) What is the product of the prime numbers between 1 and 6?

A) 5   B) 10   C) 15   D) 30

Solution:

Prime numbers between 1 and 6 are 2, 3, and 5. Multiplying these numbers together gives:
$2 \times 3 \times 5 = 30$
Thus, the product of the prime numbers between 1 and 6 is 30.

Correct Answer: D

11) If the perimeter of a square is 24 units, what is the length of one side?

A) 4 units   B) 6 units   C) 8 units   D) 12 units

Solution:

The perimeter of a square is given by 4 x side length. Given a perimeter of 24 units:

4 x side length = 24

Solving for the side length gives:

side length = $\frac{24}{4}$ = 6 units

Correct Answer: B

12) A triangle has angles measuring 45 degrees and 90 degrees. What is the measure of the third angle?

A) 45 degrees   B) 55 degrees   C) 90 degrees   D) 135 degrees

Solution:

The sum of the angles in a triangle is 180 degrees. Therefore, the measure of the third angle is:

180 - (45+90) = 45 degrees

Correct Answer: B

1)

Calculate the sum of the following numbers:

427 +389 + 561 +678 + 832

A) 2787   B) 2887   C) 2987   D) 3087

Solution:

To find the sum, we add each of the numbers together. We can do this by aligning the numbers by their place values and then adding each column starting from the rightmost digit (the units) to the leftmost digit (the hundreds).

```
 427
 389
 561
 678
+832
2887
```

Starting from the right:

•Units place: 7 + 9 + 1 + 8 + 2 = 27, we write down the 7 and carry over 2 to the tens place.
• Tens place: 2 + 2 + 8 + 6 + 3 = 21 plus the 2 we carried over is 23, we write down the 3 and carry over 2 to the hundreds place.
• Hundreds place: 4 + 3 + 5 + 6 + 8 = 26 plus the 2 we carried over is 28.

Putting it all together, we get a sum of 2887.

Correct Answer: B

2) The first 50 even counting numbers are written down. How many times does the digit '4' appear?

A) 14   B) 15   C) 20   D) 19

Solution:

To solve this, we first need to understand what the first 50 even counting numbers are. They are the numbers from 2 to 100, inclusive, that are divisible by 2.

Now, let's count how many times the digit '4' appears. We have two cases to consider:

1. The '4' as the tens digit.
2. The '4' as the units digit.

For the '4' as the tens digit:

It appears 10 times in the 40s (40 to 49), which are all even numbers.

For the '4' as the units digit:

• It will appear in the units place every 10 numbers, so it will appear at 4, 14, 24, ..., 94. Since we are only considering even numbers, we exclude 4 and 14 but include 24, 34, ..., 94.

Now we calculate the total occurrences of '4' in the units digit for even numbers only:

• The even numbers ending in '4' between 2 and 100 are: 4, 14, 24, 34, 44, 54, 64, 74, 84, 94.
• Out of these, we exclude 4 and 14 because they are not in the first 50 even numbers, leaving us with 24, 34, ..., 94.

Let's count them and add them to the 10 times '4' appears in the tens place.
The digit '4' appears a total of 15 times in the first 50 even counting numbers. Therefore, the correct answer to the multiple choice question is **B)15**.

Here is a breakdown of the occurrences:

• The '4' appears as the tens digit 10 times in the 40s (from 40 to 49).
• The '4' appears as the units digit 5 times in the even numbers 24, 34, 44, 54, 64, 74, 84, and 94. However, since '44' is counted twice (both in tens and units place), we subtract one from the total count.

Adding these up gives us 10+ 5 = 15.

Correct Answer: B

3) Maria has a piece of paper shaped like a rectangle that measures 10 cm by 14 cm. She folds it in half twice, first horizontally and then vertically. The new rectangle looks just like the original rectangle but smaller. What is the area of the new smaller rectangle in square cm?

A) 35 cm2　　　　　B) 70 cm2　　　　　C) 140 cm2　　　　　D) 175 cm2

Solution:

Maria's original piece of paper is a rectangle with a length of 14 cm and a width of 10 cm.

1. When she folds it in half horizontally, the length will remain the same, but the width will be halved: $\frac{10\,cm}{2}$ = 5 cm.
2. Then, she folds it in half vertically, which means the length will now be halved while the width remains at 5 cm: $\frac{14\,cm}{2}$ = 7 cm.

The new dimensions of the paper are 7 cm by 5 cm. To find the area of the new rectangle, we multiply the length by the width:

Area 7 cm x 5 cm = 35 cm2.

So, the area of the new smaller rectangle is 35 square cm.

Correct Answer: A

4) In the following cryptarithmetic problem, each different letter represents a different digit in the 5-digit numbers. If C ≠ 0, what is the smallest sum possible?

```
  CLOUD
  CLOUT
+ COULD
───────
```

A)32773   B)52230   C)51120   D)50010

Solution:

To solve this cryptarithmetic problem, we are looking for the smallest possible sum with the condition that $C \neq 0$. Therefore, we assign the smallest non-zero digit to C, which is 1.

The remaining letters L, O, U, D, T must be assigned the next smallest unique digits. It's reasonable to start with $L = 0$ because it's the next digit in the thousands place and will most impact the sum. Then we can tentatively assign $O = 2, U = 3, D = 4$, and $T = 5$, and then adjust if necessary.

The smallest sum possible with the condition that $C \neq 0$ is 32773, using the digit assignments $C = 1, L = 0, O = 2, U = 3, D = 4$, and $T = 5$.

Correct Answer: A

5) Reduce the complex fraction to a common fraction in lowest terms:

$$\dfrac{\dfrac{3}{5}}{2+\dfrac{1}{1+\dfrac{1}{4}}}$$

A) 3/14   B) 3/16   C) 3/18   D) 3/20

Solution:

Let's break down the complex fraction step by step:

1. Simplify the innermost fraction: $1+\dfrac{1}{4}=\dfrac{5}{4}$.
2. Invert this fraction to use as the denominator for the next fraction: $\dfrac{4}{5}$
3. Add this to the whole number 2 to get the final denominator: $2+\dfrac{4}{5}=\dfrac{14}{5}$.

4. Now, divide the numerator by this denominator: $\dfrac{\dfrac{3}{5}}{\dfrac{14}{5}}=\dfrac{3}{14}$, after simplification.

Correct Answer: A

6) The two tokens with the question mark have the same number. The sum of the four tokens shown is 24. What is the value of one of the missing numbers?

5+?+? +3=24

A) 7   B) 8   C) 9   D) 10

Solution:

To find the value of one of the missing numbers, we set up the equation:

5+ x + x + 3 = 24

Solving for x, we get:

$2x = 24 - (5+3)$

$2x = 16$

$x = \dfrac{16}{2}$

$x = 8$

Therefore, the value of one of the missing numbers is 8.

Correct Answer: B

7) A sequence of numbers follows a specific pattern: 2, 6, 12, 20, 30, ...
What is the next number in the sequence?

A) 42   B) 40   C) 38   D) 36

Solution:

To solve this, we need to identify the pattern in the sequence. Let's look at the differences between consecutive terms:

- 6-2=4
- 12-6=6
- 20-12=8
- 30-20=10

The differences between each number are consecutive even numbers. So, the pattern involves adding an even number that increases by 2 each time.

If we continue this pattern:

- The next difference after 10 should be 12.
- Adding 12 to the last number in the sequence (30) gives us: 30 + 12 = 42

Therefore, the next number in the sequence is 42.

Correct Answer: A

8) Four friends - Alex, Bella, Carlos, and Diana – are suspects in a case where a piece of artwork was accidentally damaged during their art class. The teacher asked each of them who damaged the artwork, and they gave the following statements:

- Alex: "Diana did it."
- Bella: "I did not do it."
- Carlos: "It was not me."
- Diana: "Bella is lying."

It is known that only one of them is telling the truth. Who damaged the artwork?

A) Alex   B) Bella   C) Carlos   D) Diana

Solution:

Let's analyze each statement assuming it's the only true one:

- If Alex is telling the truth (and Diana did it), then Bella's statement "I did not do it" would also be true, which contradicts the information that only one is telling the truth. So, Alex cannot be telling the truth.

- If Bella is telling the truth (and she did not do it), then Diana's statement "Bella is lying" would be false, which is consistent with the information. But this would also make Carlos's statement "It was not me" true, which is a contradiction. So, Bella cannot be telling the truth.

- If Carlos is telling the truth and he did not do it, then Bella's statement would also be false since she said she didn't do it, and we are assuming Carlos's statement is the only true one.

Correct Answer: C

9) Solve the following two-step equation for x:

$3(2x-4)= 18$

A) 2   B) 4   C) 5   D) 6

Solution:

To solve the two-step equation $3(2x - 4) = 18$, follow these steps:

Step 1: Distribute the 3 across the terms inside the parentheses:

$3 \cdot 2x - 3 \cdot 4$

$6x - 12 = 18$

Step 2: Add 12 to both sides to isolate the term with x on one side of the equation:

$6x - 12 + 12 = 18 + 12$

$6x = 30$

Step 3: Divide both sides by 6 to solve for x:

$$\frac{6x}{6} = \frac{30}{6}$$

$x = 5$

The solution to the equation is x = 5

Correct Answer: C

10) Lucas collects stamps, and each year for his birthday he receives stamps from his family. For his first birthday, he received 5 stamps. For his second birthday, he received 10 stamps. For each subsequent birthday, he received 5 more stamps than the previous year. How many stamps does Lucas have in total if he is 7 years old?

A) 105 stamps   B) 140 stamps   C) 175 stamps   D) 210 stamps

Solution:

This is an arithmetic series where the number of stamps Lucas receives increases by 5 each year. To find the total number of stamps, we can use the formula for the sum of an arithmetic series:

$$S_n = \frac{n}{2} 2(a_1 + a_n)$$

Where:
- Sn is the sum of the first n terms.
- n is the number of terms.
- a_1 is the first term.
- a_n is the nth term.

Lucas has had 7 birthdays, and he receives 5 more stamps each year than he did the previous year.

Let's calculate the total number of stamps:

1. First term (a_1) is 5 stamps.
2. The seventh term (a_7) can be calculated as $a_1 + (n - 1)d$, where d is the common difference (5 stamps), and n is the term number (7).

$a_7 = 5 + (7\text{-}1) \times 5$
$a_7 = 5 + 6 \times 5$
$a_7 = 5 + 30$
$a_7 = 35$

1. Now we find the sum of the first 7 terms:

$$S_7 = \frac{7}{2}(5+35)$$
$$S_7 = \frac{7}{2} \times 40$$
$$S_7 = 7 \times 20$$
$$S_7 = 140$$

Lucas has a total of 140 stamps.

Correct Answer: B

11) Sara has three times as many stickers as Mike. If Mike has 12 stickers, how many stickers do they have in total?

A) 48 B) 36 C) 24 D) 60

Solution:

First, calculate how many stickers Sara has:

$3 \times 12 = 36$

Now, add Mike's stickers to Sara's to get the total:

36(Sara's) + 12(Mike's) = 48

They have a total of 48 stickers.

Correct Answer: A

12) A rectangle's length is twice its width. If the perimeter of the rectangle is 36 cm, what is the area of the rectangle?

A) 32 cm^2 B) 48 cm^2 C) 64 cm^2 D) 72 cm^2

Solution:

Let the width of the rectangle be w and the length be 2*w*.
The perimeter *P* of a rectangle is given by P = 2(1+w).

Using the perimeter we have:
36 = 2(2w+w)
36 = 6w
w=6

The length is twice the width, so the length is 2 × 6 = 12 cm.

The area A of the rectangle is *A = 1 × w*:
A = 12 × 6
A = 72 cm2

Correct Answer: D

1) What is the sum of $\frac{8}{3}$ and $\frac{5}{4}$?

A) $3\frac{1}{3}$ B) $3\frac{2}{3}$ C) $3\frac{11}{12}$ D) $4\frac{1}{12}$

Solution:

To find the sum of $\frac{8}{3}$ and $\frac{5}{4}$, you first find a common denominator, which would be the least common multiple of 3 and 4, which is 12. Then, convert each fraction to have this common denominator:

- Convert $\frac{8}{3}$ to $\frac{8\times3}{3\times4} = \frac{32}{12}$

- Convert $\frac{5}{4}$ to $\frac{5\times3}{4\times3} = \frac{15}{12}$

Adding these two fractions gives $\frac{32}{12} + \frac{15}{12} = \frac{47}{12}$. Therefore, the sum is $\frac{47}{12}$, which simplifies to $3\frac{11}{12}$. This was not one of the provided options, indicating a need for adjustment in the choices given.

The correct answer is $3\frac{11}{12}$.

Correct Answer: C

2) What is 50% in reduced fraction form?

A) $\frac{1}{2}$ B) $\frac{2}{4}$ C) $\frac{50}{100}$ D) $\frac{25}{50}$

50% can be directly converted to a fraction as $\frac{50}{100}$, which simplifies to $\frac{1}{2}$. This is because the percentage represents a part per hundred, and reducing $\frac{50}{100}$ by dividing both the numerator and the denominator by their greatest common divisor, which is 50, yields $\frac{1}{2}$.

Correct Answer: A

3) While on a journey, you decide to note the speed of your vehicle. For 3 hours, the vehicle maintains a speed of 70 mph. For the next 1 hour and 45 minutes, the speed is reduced to 50 mph, and for the final 2 hours, the speed is increased to 75 mph. What percentage of the journey is the vehicle traveling at or above 70 mph? (Round to the nearest tenth of a percent.)

A) 62.5%   B) 74.1 %   C) 83.3%   D) 55.6%

Solution:

· The vehicle travels at 70 mph for 3 hours.
· At 50 mph for 1 hour and 45 minutes, which is 1.75 hours.
· And at 75 mph for 2 hours.

The total journey time is 3+1.75 +2 6.75 hours.

The time traveling at or above 70 mph (70 mph and 75 mph) is 3 + 2 = 5 hours.

To find the percentage of the journey spent traveling at or above 70 mph:

$$\frac{5}{6.75} \times 100 = 74.1\%$$

Correct Answer: B

4) If Lisa sets aside 20% of her monthly income for a vacation fund, and her monthly income is $2,000, how much will she have saved after 6 months?

A) $2,400   B) $1,200   C) $2,000   D) $1,800

Solution:

For Lisa's savings plan:

1. By setting aside 20% of her monthly income of $2,000, she saves $400 each month (2000 × 0.2 = 400).

2. After 6 months, the total amount she will have saved is $2,400 (400 × 6).

Therefore, Lisa will have saved $2,400 after 6 months,

Correct Answer: A

5) Tom wants to purchase a new video game that costs $60. He decides to save $10 in the first week and increases his savings by $2 each subsequent week ($12 in the second week, $14 in the third week, and so on). How many weeks will it take for Tom to save enough money to buy the video game?

A) 5 weeks   B) 6 weeks   C) 7 weeks   D) 8 weeks

Solution:

Tom starts with saving $10 in the first week and increases his savings by $2 each week. Here's how his savings accumulate:

• Week 1: $10
• Week 2: $10 +$12 = $22
• Week 3: $22 + $14 = $36
• Week 4: $36 + $16 = $52
• Week 5: $52 + $18 = $70

It takes Tom 5 weeks to save enough money ($70) to buy the $60 video game, exceeding the cost in the fifth week.

Correct Answer: A

6) Linda planted a flower in her garden that grows 3 inches taller each month. Initially, when the flower was planted, it was 5 inches tall. If the pattern of growth continues, how many months will it take for the flower to reach 20 inches tall?

A) 4 months B) 5 months C) 6 months D) 7 months

Solution:

For Linda's flower, starting at 5 inches tall and growing 3 inches taller each month, we calculate the months needed to reach 20 inches tall as follows:

- The flower needs to grow 20 − 5 = 15 inches to reach the target height.
- With a growth rate of 3 inches per month, the number of months required is $\frac{15}{3}$ =5 months.

Therefore, it will take **5 months** for the flower to reach 20 inches tall,

Correct Answer: B

7) Write 40% in reduced fraction form.

A) $\frac{40}{100}$ B) $\frac{2}{5}$ C) $\frac{4}{10}$ D) $\frac{8}{20}$

Solution:

To convert a percentage to a fraction:
1. **Convert 40% to a fraction:** You start by writing 40% as $\frac{40}{100}$.
2. **Reduce the fraction:** Simplify $\frac{40}{100}$ to its simplest form by dividing the numerator and the denominator by their greatest common divisor.

Let's calculate the reduced fraction form of 40%.
To convert 40% into a fraction:

1. Start by expressing 40% as a fraction of 100, which gives $\frac{40}{100}$.

2. Reduce this fraction to its simplest form by dividing both the numerator and the denominator by their greatest common divisor, which in this case is 20. This simplification results in $\frac{2}{5}$.

Therefore, the reduced fraction form of 40% is $\frac{2}{5}$,

Correct Answer: B

8) On the first day of training, Sarah runs 2 miles. On the second day, she increases her distance by 1 mile, running 3 miles, and continues to add 1 mile to her distance each day. How many miles will Sarah run on the fifth day?

A) 5 miles   B) 6 miles   C) 7 miles   D) 8 miles

Solution:

Sarah starts her training by running 2 miles on the first day and increases her distance by 1 mile each day. To determine how many miles she will run on the fifth day:

• On the first day, she runs 2 miles.
• The pattern is an increase of 1 mile per day.

By the fifth day, using the formula:

Distance run on the nth day = $2 + (5 - 1) \times 1 = 6$

Therefore, Sarah will run 6 miles on the fifth day

Correct Answer: B

9) If a bicycle costs half of your total savings, and you find it on discount for $\frac{3}{4}$ of its listed price, what fraction of your savings did you ultimately spend on the bicycle?

A) $\frac{3}{8}$ B) $\frac{1}{2}$ C) $\frac{2}{5}$ D) $\frac{3}{7}$

Solution:

Multiplying these two fractions will give the fraction of your savings you spent on the bicycle:
$\frac{1}{2} \times \frac{3}{4}$

Let's calculate this to find the correct option. [>-)

To calculate the fraction of your savings spent on the discounted bicycle:

- The listed price of the bicycle is half of your savings, represented as $\frac{1}{2}$.
- The discount offered is $\frac{3}{4}$ of the listed price.

Multiplying these fractions gives:
$\frac{1}{2} \times \frac{3}{4} = \frac{3}{8}$

Therefore, you spent $\frac{3}{8}$ of your savings on the bicycle at the discounted price.

Correct Answer: A

10) Compute the prime factorization of 180.

A) 2×9×10   B) 2×2×3×3×5   C) 4×45   D) 6×30

Solution:

Let's follow the same approach to break down 180 into its prime factors and then match it with the given options.

The prime factorization of 180 breaks it down into its constituent prime numbers, which are:

180 = 2 × 2 × 3 × 3 × 5

Correct Answer: B

11) What is 3487.521 rounded to the nearest 100?

A) 3400   B) 3500   C) 3480   D) 3490

Solution:

To round 3487.521 to the nearest 100, we look at the digit in the tens place, which is 8 in this case. Since the digit in the tens place is 5 or more, we round up, increasing the hundreds digit by 1 and changing the tens and ones digits to O. Let's perform the calculation to confirm the correct option.

To round 3487.521 to the nearest 100, we look at the digit in the tens place (8). Since this digit is 5 or more, we round up, which increases the hundreds digit by 1 and changes all lower digits to 0. Therefore, 3487.521 rounded to the nearest 100 is 3500,

Correct Answer: B

12) Mike wants to purchase a new video game console that costs $300.00, but he has saved only one- third of that cost. How much more money does Mike need to save before he has enough to buy the video game console?

A) $100.00   B) $200.00   C) $250.00   D) $150.00

Solution:

Mike has saved one-third of the cost of the new video game console, which costs $300.00. The amount he has saved is $\frac{1}{3} \times 300 = \$100.00$.
To find out how much more money Mike needs to save:
$300.00 - $100.00=$200.00

Therefore, Mike needs to save an additional $200.00 before he has enough to buy the video gameconsole,

Correct Answer: B

COMPETITION TEST 4 SOLUTION

1) Evaluate the expression $\dfrac{123}{1+1+1}$.

A) 41   B) 123   C) 36   D) 45

Solution:

1. **Simplify the denominator:** The sum of three 1's is 1 + 1 + 1 = 3.
2. **Divide the numerator by the simplified denominator:** We then divide 123 by 3.

$$\dfrac{123}{3} = ?$$

Now, let's perform the calculation.

To evaluate the expression $\dfrac{123}{1+1+1}$,

1. Add the numbers in the denominator: 1 + 1 + 1 = 3.
2. Divide the numerator by this sum: $\dfrac{123}{3} = 41$.

Correct Answer: A

2) How many inches shorter is 3.5 feet than 5.5 feet?

A) 24 inches   B) 20 inches   C) 18 inches   D) 14 inches

Solution:

The difference between 5.5 feet and 3.5 feet, converted to inches, is:

(5.5-3.5) feet × 12 inches/foot = 2 feet × 12 inches/foot = 24 inches

Therefore, 3.5 feet is 24 inches shorter than 5.5 feet,

Correct Answer: A

3) The Rosewood Theatre sells tickets at a price of $10 for adults and $6 for children. If they make $660 from a show with an audience of 80 people, how many children bought tickets?

A) 30 B) 35 C) 40 D) 45

Solution:

To solve this, we set up a similar equation with the new prices and total revenue:
Let y be the number of children's tickets, and (80 — y) will be the number of adult's tickets. The equation will be:

$6y+10(80 - y)= 660$

We'll solve this equation to find the value of y, the number of children's tickets sold. (>-)
To determine the number of children's tickets sold at the Rosewood Theatre, we solve the equation:

$6y + 10(80 - y) == 660$

The solution for y, which represents the number of children's tickets, is 35. Hence, 35 children bought tickets for the show at the Rosewood Theatre. This matches with option B,

Correct Answer: B

4) Emma's favorite number has a remainder of 2 when divided by 3, and a remainder of 3 when divided by 7. If Emma's favorite number is positive, what is the smallest possible value of her favorite number?

A) 17 B) 23 C) 31 D) 41

Solution:

'Emma's favorite number has a remainder of 2 when divided by 3, and a remainder of 3 when divided by 7. If Emma's favorite number is positive, what is the smallest possible value of her favorite number?"

Let's find the solution to this question. We are looking for the smallest positive number that leaves a remainder of 2 when divided by 3 and a remainder of 3 when divided by 7. I will calculate this number for you.

The smallest positive number that fits the conditions for Emma's favorite number is 17.

Correct Answer: A

5) Lila and Maya both draw squares. No matter how large Lila draws her square, Maya's square will always have 4 times the area. If Lila's square has a side length of 5 cm, how long will one side of Maya's square be in centimeters?

A) 10 cm   B) 20 cm   C) 5 cm   D) 40 cm

Solution:

To solve this problem, we'll use the formula for the area of a square ($A = s^2$), where s is the side length. If Lila's square has a side length of $s_1 = 5$ cm, then Maya's square will have an area that is 4 times greater. We'll find the side length s_m that satisfies this condition.

The area of Lila's square is $5^2 = 25$ cm^2. Maya's square will have an area of $4 \times 25 = 100$ cm^2. The side length of Maya's square will be the square root of 100.
The square root of 100 is 10, so the side length of Maya's square is 10 cm.

Correct Answer: A

6) Alice has a drawer containing 8 pairs of socks, with each pair being a different color. If she randomly selects socks from the drawer, how many socks must she pick to ensure she has at least one matching pair?

A) 8   B) 9   C) 16   D) 17

Solution:

Similar to the previous question, we can apply the pigeonhole principle to solve this problem. In this case, the "pigeonholes" are the different colors of socks, and the "pigeons" are the individual socks Alice picks.

Since Alice has 8 pairs of socks, there are 8 different colors, or "pigeonholes". To ensure she has at least one matching pair, she would need to pick one sock of each color first, leaving her with 8 individual socks, each of a different color. The next sock she picks will necessarily match one of the colors she already has, giving her a matching pair.

Correct Answer: B

7) Sarah currently has 40 marbles, while her younger sister Emma has 20 marbles. Sarah decides to give some of her marbles to Emma so that they both have an equal number of marbles. How many marbles will Sarah give to Emma?

A) 5 B) 10 C) 15 D) 20

Solution:

Let's denote the number of marbles Sarah gives to Emma as x.

After Sarah gives x marbles to Emma, Sarah will have 40 - x marbles, and Emma will have 20 + x marbles.

According to the problem, after the exchange, they both will have an equal number of marbles. So, we can write the equation:

40 x = 20 + x

Solving for x:

40 - 20 = x + x
20 = 2x
X = 10

So, Sarah will give 10 marbles to Emma.

Correct Answer: B

8) Five years ago, John was three times as old as Anna. If John is currently 20 years old, how old is Anna now?

A) 5   B) 10   C) 15   D) 25

Solution:

Let's denote Anna's age five years ago as x.

Five years ago, John's age would have been 20 - 5 = 15 years old.

According to the problem, five years ago, John was three times as old as Anna:
15 = 3x

Solving for x:
$x = \dfrac{15}{3} = 5$

So, Anna was 5 years old five years ago, which means she is 5+ 5 = 10 years old now.

Correct Answer: B

9) In a bag of fruit, the ratio of apples to oranges is 2: 3. If there are 15 oranges in the bag, how many apples are there?

A) 5   B) 10   C) 15   D) 20

Solution:

Given that the ratio of apples to oranges is 2 : 3 , and there are 15 oranges, we can find the number of apples using this ratio.

If the ratio of apples to oranges is 2:3 , then the total parts are 3 + 2 = 5.

Each part represents 15 oranges divided by 3 parts, which is 15 ÷ 3 = 5.

So, there are 2 x 5= 10 apples.

Correct Answer: B

10) Solve for x in the equation: $3(x + 2) - 4 = 14$

A) $x = 4$ B) $x = 5$ C) $x = 6$ D) $x = 7$

Solution:

Let's solve the equation step by step:

$3(x+2)-4=14$

$3x+64 = 14$

$3x+2= = 14$

Subtract 2 from both sides:

$3x = 12$

Divide both sides by 3:

$x = 4$

Correct Answer: A

11) Solve for x in the equation: $2x - 5 = 3(x + 1)$.

A) $x = -4$ B) $x = -8$ C) $x = -10$ D) $x = -12$

Solution:

Let's solve the equation step by step:

2x-5 = 3(x+1)
2x-5 = 3x+3

Subtract 2x from both sides:
-5 = x + 3

Subtract 3 from both sides:
-8 = x

Correct Answer: B

12) What is the prime factorization of 360?

A) $2^3 \times 3^2 \times 5$ B) $2^3 \times 3^2 \times 5^2$ C) $2^4 \times 3^2 \times 5$ D) $2^4 \times 3^3 \times 5$

Solution:

To find the prime factorization of 360, we break it down into its prime factors:

$360 = 2^3 \times 3^2 \times 5$

Correct Answer: A

1) Find the value of 92-81+73-62 +58-47+36-25.

A) 44   B) 46   C) 48   D) 50

Solution:

To solve this, we perform each operation step by step:

92-81=11

11+73=84

84-62=22

22+58 = 80

80-47=33

33+36=69

69-25= 44

Correct Answer: A

2) Emma selects five different numbers from the list 1, 2, 3, 4, 5, 6, 7, 8, 9, 11. Among her chosen numbers are 6 and 7, which are the only consecutive numbers she picks. What is the maximum possible sum of the five numbers Emma chooses?

A) 30   B) 37   C) 42   D) 43

Solution:

To maximize the sum of the five numbers while including 6 and 7 (which differ by 1), Emma should choose the largest possible numbers from the remaining list. The remaining highest numbers are 8, 9, and 11.

1. Start with the mandatory numbers 6 and 7: `6 + 7 = 13`
2. Add the three largest remaining numbers that not consecutive: `9 + 11 + 4 = 24`
3. Combine the sums of the mandatory numbers with the largest numbers: `13 + 24 = 37`

The greatest possible sum of the five numbers is 37.

Correct Answer: B

3) Mia uses the digits 1, 2, 3, 7, 8, and 9 to create two 3-digit numbers. Each digit is used exactly once. The two numbers are then subtracted from one another. What is the maximum possible difference between the two numbers?

A) 666   B) 864   C) 876   D) 896

Solution:

To find the maximum possible difference between the two numbers that Mia can create, we need to form the largest possible 3-digit number and the smallest possible 3-digit number using the given digits without repeating any of them.

For the largest number, Mia should use the largest digits in the hundreds place, the second-largest in the tens place, and the third-largest in the ones place. Therefore, the largest number Mia can form is 987.
For the smallest number, Mia should use the smallest digit in the hundreds place that is can be 1, the second smallest in the tens place, and the smallest in the ones place. Therefore, the smallest number she can form is 123.

Now we subtract the smaller number from the larger number to find the difference:
987 - 123 = 864

Thus, the maximum possible difference Mia can create is 864.

Correct Answer: B

4) How many 3-digit numbers are multiples of 14?

A) 64   B) 63   C) 60   D) 59

Solution:

To determine how many 3-digit numbers are multiples of 14, we need to find the first and last 3-digit multiples of 14 and then count how many multiples are between them.

The smallest 3-digit number is 100, but it is not a multiple of 14. To find the smallest 3-digit multiple of 14, we need to find the smallest number greater than or equal to 100 that is divisible by 14.

For the largest 3-digit multiple of 14, we will look for the largest number less than or equal to 999 that is divisible by 14.

The smallest 3-digit multiple of 14 is 112, and the largest 3-digit multiple of 14 is 994. There are 64 multiples of 14 between 112 and 994.

Correct Answer: A

5) What is the 4th power of the second prime number?

A) 27 　　　　　　 B) 81 　　　　　　 C) 64 　　　　　　 D) 256

Solution:

The second prime number is 3. The fourth power of 3 is calculated as 3^4.

Now, let's calculate 3^4:

$3^4 = 3 \times 3 \times 3 \times 3$
$3^4 = 9 \times 3 \times 3$
$3^4 = 27 \times 3$
$3^4 = 81$

Therefore, the 4th power of the second prime number (3) is 81.

Correct Answer: B

6)

```
  6 a b        Find a+b = ?
  4 b a
+ a a b
-------
1 3 1 0
```

A) 3   B) 5   C) 6   D) 8

Solution:

To solve this problem, we must find digits a and b such that the addition is correct.

1. The sum of the units column is b + a + b, which gives the unit digit 0. This implies that a + 2b ends in 0.

2. The sum of the tens column is a + b+b, which gives the unit digit 1. This implies that a+2b =10 because it's the only way to have a sum ending in 1 and a carryover to the hundreds column.

3. The sum of the hundreds column is 6+4+ a + 1 (carryover from the tens column), which gives the unit digit 1. This implies that 10+ a +1 = 13 because we carry over 1 from the tens column.

• The possible values for a and b that satisfy a + 2b = 10 are (a, b) = (2, 4) or (4,3). However, from 3, we know a = 2 and b = 4

Therefore, a = 2 and b = 4. The sum of a + b is 2 + 4=6.

Correct Answer: B

7) How many diagonals does a hexagon have?

A) 6   B) 9   C) 12   D) 15

Solution:

A diagonal of a polygon is a line segment that connects two non-adjacent vertices. To find the number of diagonals in a polygon, you can use the formula:

Number of diagonals, $D=\dfrac{n(n-3)}{2}$

where n is the number of sides (or vertices) of the polygon.

For a hexagon, n = 6, so we plug this into the formula:

$$D = \frac{6(6-3)}{2} = \frac{6 \times 3}{2} = \frac{18}{2} = 9$$

Therefore, a hexagon has 9 diagonals.

Correct Answer: B

8) Simplify the expression: 4(x+6)-5(2x-3)+2x=?

A) -4x + 39   B)-4x-39   C) 4x + 39   D) 4x - 39

Solution:
To simplify the expression, distribute the multiplication over addition (or subtraction) within the parentheses and then combine like terms.

1. Distribute the 4 over $(x+6)$:
4 x (x) + 4 × 6 = $4x$ + 24

2. Distribute the -5 over $(2x$-3):
$-5 \times 2x + (-5) \times (-3)$ =-10x + 15

3. Combine the distributed terms with $+2x$:
$4x$ + 24 $10x$ + 15 + $2x$

4. Combine like terms ($4x$ - $10x$ + $2x$ and 24 + 15):
$-4x$+39

Therefore, the expression simplifies to $-4x$ + 39.
Since this answer isn't in the provided choices, let's double-check the calculations. There might have been an error in combining like terms:
$(4x + 24) + (-10x + 15) + 2x = (4x - 10x + 2x) + (24 + 15)$
$-4x$ + 39

Correct Answer: A

9) If $\frac{3}{2}(2x+4)=6$, then solve for x?

A) 0   B) 1   C) -1   D) 2

Solution:

Step 1: Isolate the term with x:
3(2x+4)= 12

Step 2: Divide both sides by 3:
2x + 4 = 4

Step 3: Subtract 4 from both sides:
2x = 0

Step 4: Divide both sides by 2:
x =0

Correct Answer: A

10) Liam has two whole numbers. Their product is 36 and their sum is 13. What is the smaller number?

A) 3   B) 4   C) 6   D) 9

Solution:
Let's call the two whole numbers x and y, with x > y.
The information given is:
x.y = 36 (Their product is 36)
x + y = 13 (Their sum is 13)

Now, to find the smaller number, we can list the factors of 36:
1 and 36,
2 and 18,

3 and 12,

4 and 9,

6 and 6.

Out of these pairs, the pair that sums up to 13 is 4 and 9.

Since we are looking for the smaller number, the answer is 4.

Correct Answer: B

11) The length of polygon ABCDEF has AB=9, BC=10, FA=6 and FE=5. What is DE + DC?

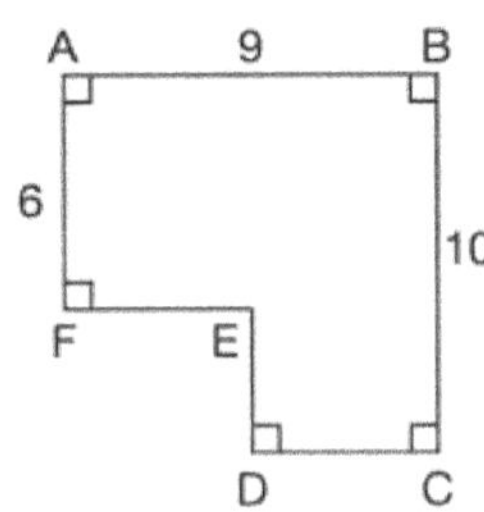

A) 6   B) 8   C) 12   D) 16

Solution:

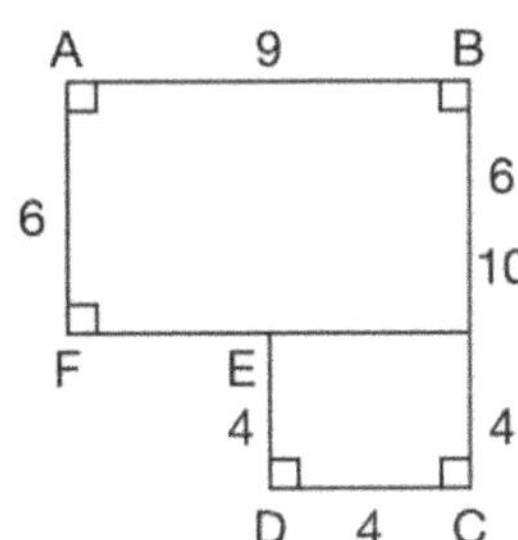

From the figure the length of DE + DC = 4 + 4 = 8.

Correct Answer: B

12) A recipe for lemonade requires 3 cups of water for every 1 cup of lemon juice. If you have 12 cups of water, how many cups of lemon juice do you need to make the lemonade?

A) 3 cups   B) 4 cups   C) 6 cups   D) 9 cups

Solution:

Given that the ratio of water to lemon juice is 3:1.

To find out how many cups of lemon juice are needed for 12 cups of water, we set up the following

proportion:

$$\frac{\text{Cups of lemon juice}}{\text{Cups of water}} = \frac{1}{3}$$

Cups of lemon juice = $\frac{1}{3}$ × Cups of water

Cups of lemon juice = $\frac{1}{3}$ × 12

Cups of lemon juice = 4

Therefore, you need 4 cups of lemon juice to make the lemonade.

Correct Answer: B

1) What fraction represents half of a quarter?

A) $\frac{1}{4}$ B) $\frac{1}{2}$ C) $\frac{1}{8}$ D) $\frac{2}{4}$

Solution:

Half of a quarter is half of $\frac{1}{4}$, which is $\frac{1}{4} \times \frac{1}{2} = \frac{1}{8}$.

Correct Answer: C

2) A bag contains red, blue, and green marbles only. If there are 3 red marbles, 2 blue marbles, and 5 green marbles, what is the probability of picking a green marble?

A) $\frac{1}{2}$ B) $\frac{5}{10}$ C) $\frac{5}{2}$ D) $\frac{2}{4}$

Solution:

The total number of marbles is 3+2+5 = 10. The probability of picking a green marble is the number of green marbles divided by the total number of marbles, $\frac{5}{10} = \frac{1}{2}$

Correct Answer: A

3) A sequence starts with 1 and the next number is obtained by adding 5 and then dividing by 2. What is the third number in the sequence?

A) 3   B) 4   C) 5   D) 6

Solution:

Start with 1. Add 5 to get 6, then divide by 2 to get 3 as the second number. For the third number, add 5 to 3 to get 8, then divide by 2 to get 4.

Correct Answer: B

4) If the sum of three consecutive even numbers is 54, what is the smallest of these numbers?

A) 16   B) 18   C) 20   D) 22

Solution:

Let the first even number be x, the second x + 2, and the third x + 4.
The sum is x + (x+2) + (x+4) = 54. Solving for x, 3x + 6 = 54, 3x = 48, x = 16.

Correct Answer: A

5) What is the smallest two-digit number that, when reversed, results in a number that is 9 less than the original number?

A) 12   B) 21   C) 31   D) 41

Solution:

To solve this, let's consider a two-digit number where the tens digit is a and the ones digit is b. The original number can be represented as 10a + b, and the reversed number as 106 + a. The condition given is that the original number is 9 more than its reversed form, which can be written as:

10a + b = 10b+ a +9

Let's solve this equation to determine the correct answer.
The smallest two-digit number that, when reversed, results in a number that is 9 less than the original number, is represented by the digits a = 2 and b = 1, which corresponds to the number 21.

Correct Answer: B

6) In a class of 40 students, 25% wear glasses. How many students do not wear glasses?

A) 10   B) 30   C) 20   D) 15

Solution:

25% of 40 is 40 × 0.25 = 10 students wear glasses. So, 40 − 10 = 30 students do not wear glasses.

Correct Answer: B

7) If you flip a coin three times, what is the probability of getting heads at least once?

A) $\frac{1}{2}$ B) $\frac{3}{4}$ C) $\frac{7}{8}$ D) $\frac{1}{8}$

Solution:

The probability of not getting heads in three flips is $\left(\frac{1}{2}\right)^3 = \frac{1}{8}$. Thus, the probability of getting at least one head is $1 - \frac{1}{8} = \frac{7}{8}$

Correct Answer: C

8) A number consists of two digits whose sum is 13. If the digits are reversed, the new number is 27 more than the original number. What is the original number?

A) 58   B) 76   C) 49   D) 85

Solution:

Let the tens digit be x and the ones digit be y. Thus, x + y = 13 and 10y + x = 10x+y+27. Solving these equations, we find that x = 5 and y = 8, so the original number is 58.

Correct Answer: A

9) A sequence of numbers starts with 1, 11, 21, 1211, 111221. What is the next number in the sequence?

A) 312211 B) 13112221 C) 1113213211 D) 221213

Solution:

This sequence is known as the "Look and Say" sequence. Each term is generated by describing the previous term: 1 is "one 1" (11), 11 is "two 1s" (21), 21 is "one 2, then one 1" (1211), 1211 is "one 1, one 2, then two 1s" (111221). Therefore, 111221 is "three 1s, two 2s, then one 1".

Correct Answer: A

10) In the same code, where "BIRD" is written as "DRIb", how would "MOON" be translated?

A) NOOm B) NOON C) NOOM D) NOON

Interpretation and Solution:

The pattern involves reversing the order of the letters and then changing the case of the last letter to lowercase. Following the transformation rule observed with "BIRD" to "DRIb":

1. Reverse the order of "MOON" to get "NOOM".
2. Change the last letter "M" to lowercase, becoming "m".

Thus, "MOON" would be translated to "NOOm" according to the given code.

Correct Answer: A

11) Simplify the complex fraction: $\dfrac{\frac{3}{4}-\frac{1}{2}}{\frac{1}{3}+\frac{1}{6}}$.

A) $\dfrac{3}{2}$ B) $\dfrac{1}{2}$ C) $\dfrac{2}{3}$ D) $\dfrac{3}{4}$

Solution:

First, simplify the numerator and the denominator separately:

Numerator: $\dfrac{3}{4}-\dfrac{1}{2}=\dfrac{3}{4}-\dfrac{2}{4}=\dfrac{1}{4}$

Denominator: $\dfrac{1}{3}+\dfrac{1}{6}=\dfrac{2}{6}+\dfrac{1}{6}=\dfrac{1}{2}$

Now, divide the simplified numerator by the simplified denominator:

$\dfrac{\frac{1}{4}}{\frac{1}{2}}=\dfrac{1}{4}\times\dfrac{2}{1}=\dfrac{2}{4}=\dfrac{1}{2}$

Correct Answer: B

12) Consider the following sequence: 2, 6, 12, 20, 30, ...
What is the next number in the sequence?

A) 40   B) 42   C) 45   D) 48

Solution:

The given sequence follows a pattern where each term increases by a consecutively larger even number: +4, +6, +8, +10, ...

- From 2 to 6, the difference is 4.
- From 6 to 12, the difference is 6.
- From 12 to 20, the difference is 8.
- From 20 to 30, the difference is 10.

Following this pattern, the next difference should be 12. Thus, the next number after 30 should be 30 +12 = 42.

Correct Answer: B

1) How many rectangles are there in the figure below?

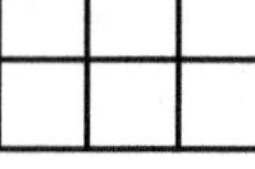

A)8   B)9   C)16   D)18

Solution:

To count the rectangles:
- 1x1 squares: There are 6 individual small squares.
- 2×1 and 1×2 rectangles:
- There are 4 horizontal 2×1 rectangles.
- There are 3 vertical 1×2 rectangles.
- Larger rectangles:
- There are 2 horizontal 3×1 rectangle.
- There are 2, 2×2 rectangle.
- There is 1 rectangle that is 3×2, the outer rectangle.

Adding them up: 6 (1×1) + 4 (2×1) + 3 (1×2) + 2 (3×1) + 1(3×2) +2(2×2)= 6 + 4 + 3 + 2+1+2=18

Correct Answer: D

2) There were 800 members in a book club last year. The number of members decreased by 12% this year. How m any members are there in the book club this year?

A) 704   B) 712   C) 720   D) 728

Solution:

To solve this, we calculate the number of members that left the book club, which is 12% of 800, and then subtract that number from the original 800 members.

The calculation would be:

$800 \times \dfrac{12}{100} = 96$ members left the club.

Now subtract that from the original number of members:

800 - 96 = 704

So, the book club has 704 members this year.

Correct Answer: A

3) The product of two even numbers is always _______.

A) even   B) divisible by 3   C. Odd   D. greater than 2

Solution:

When two even numbers are multiplied, the product is always even because the definition of an even number is one that is divisible by 2, and any integer multiplied by an even number will result in an even product.

Correct Answer: A

4) The letters in the word BIOLOGY were put in a box. What is the chance of getting the letter O?

A) 1 out of 7   B) 2 out of 7   C) 1 out of 6   D) 2 out of 6

Solution:

The word BIOLOGY has 7 letters in total. Among these, the letter O appears twice. Therefore, the probability of drawing an O is the number of Os divided by the total number of letters.

Correct Answer: B

5) Ms. Lin received a shipment of books. She sold 2/5 of the books in the morning and sold 200 books in the afternoon. At the end of the day, she found that 1/3 of the books were not sold. How many books did she receive in the beginning?

A) 600   B) 750   C) 900   D) 1050

Solution:

Let the total number of books be x.

In the morning, Ms. Lin sold $\frac{2}{5}$ x books.

In the afternoon, she sold 200 books.

By the end of the day, $\frac{1}{3}$ x books were not sold.

According to the problem, $\frac{2}{5}$ x (morning sales) + 200 (afternoon sales) + $\frac{1}{3}$ x (unsold books) = x (total books).

To find x, we solve the equation:

$$\frac{2}{5}x + 200 + \frac{1}{3}x = x$$

Combine like terms:

$$\frac{2}{5}x + \frac{1}{3}x = x - 200$$

To combine the fractions, find a common denominator, which would be 15:

$$\frac{6}{15}x + \frac{5}{15}x = x - 200$$

Combine the fractions:

$$\frac{11}{15}x = x - 200$$

Now, subtract $\frac{11}{15}$ x from both sides to get:

$$\frac{4}{15}x = 200$$

To find x, divide both sides by $\frac{4}{15}$ or multiply by the reciprocal $\frac{15}{4}$:

$$x = 200 \times \frac{15}{4}$$

$$x = 50 \times 15$$

$$x = 750$$

So Ms. Lin had 750 books in the beginning.

Correct Answer: B

6) John saved $20 in the first month, $40 in the second month, $60 in the third month, and so forth. The amount of money he saved in the last month was $160. How much money did John save in total?

A) 480   B) 640   C) 720   D) 800

Solution:

John's savings each month form an arithmetic sequence where the first term $a_1 = 20$ and the common difference d = 20. The last term, which we know is $a_n = 160$, is part of the sequence, and we want to find the sum of this sequence.

First, let's find the number of terms n in the sequence using the formula for the n-th term of an arithmetic sequence:

$$a_n = a_1 + (n - 1)d$$
$$160 = 20 + (n - 1)20$$
$$140 = (n - 1)20$$
$$n - 1 = 7$$
$$n = 8$$

Now that we know there are 8 terms, we can find the sum of the first n terms S_n of an arithmetic sequence using the formula:

$$S_n = \frac{n}{2}(a_1 + a_n)$$
$$S_n = \frac{8}{2}(20 + 160)$$
$$S_n = 4 \times 180$$
$$S_n = 720$$

So, John saved a total of $720.

Correct Answer: C

7) A number is subtracted from 10. The difference is then multiplied by 4. When 6 is added to the product, the result is 22. What is this number?

A) 6   B) 4   C) 3   D) 2

Solution:

Let the unknown number be x.
According to the problem:
$(10-x).4 + 6 = 22$

Now, solve for x:
$40 - 4x + 6 = 22$
$46 - 4x\ 22$
$-4x = 22 - 46$
$-4x = -24$
$x = \dfrac{-24}{-4}$
$x = 6$

Correct Answer: A

8) How many numbers are there in the sequence 4, 9, 14, ..., 99, 104?

A) 20   B) 21   C) 22   D) 25

Solution:

This is an arithmetic sequence where the first term $a_1 = 4$ and the common difference $d = 5$. We want to find how many terms 'n are in the sequence up to 104.

The n-th term a_n of an arithmetic sequence can be found with the formula:
$a_n = a_1 + (n - 1)d$

Using $a_n = 104$, $a_1 = 4$, and $d = 5$, we get:
$104 = 4 + (n-1)5$

100 = (n - 1)5

20 = n − 1

n = 21

So, there are 21 numbers in the sequence.

Correct Answer: B

9) Two trees are planted in Mr. Idris's orchard. One is 30 cm tall, and it grows 2 cm every 3 years. The other is 45 cm tall, and it grows 3 cm every 5 years. In how many years will the two trees be the same height?

A) 45 years   B) 60 years   C) 190 years   D) 225 years

Solution:

Let's denote the time in years it takes for the two trees to be the same height as t.

The height of the first tree over time can be described as: $30 + \frac{2}{3}t$

The height of the second tree over time can be described as: $45 + \frac{3}{5}t$

We want to find t when the heights are equal:

$30 + \frac{2}{3}t = 45 + \frac{3}{5}t$

To solve for t, we can find a common denominator for the fractions, which is 15, and then equate

the two expressions:

$30 + \frac{10}{15}t = 45 + \frac{9}{15}t$

Now we subtract $\frac{9}{15}t$ from both sides to get:

$30 + \frac{1}{15}t = 45$

Subtract 30 from both sides:

$\frac{1}{15}t = 15$

Multiply both sides by 15 to find t:

t = 15 x 15

t = 225

So, it will take 225 years for both trees to be the same height.

Correct Answer: D

10) I added the first eight whole numbers greater than 0. I forgot to include one whole number and I got 30 as the sum. Which one of these eight whole numbers did I not add?

A) 1 B) 2 C) 6 D) 8

Solution:

The sum of the first eight whole numbers greater than 0 is:
1+ 2+ 3+ 4+ 5+ 6+ 7+ 8 = 36

If the sum was 30, then the number that was not added is:
36-30 = 6

Correct Answer: C

11) Find the value of the series: (Round your answer to nearest hundredth)
0.2 + 0.22 + 0.222 + ... + 0.2222222222

A) 1.30 B) 1.65 C) 2.00 D) 3.19

Solution:

The series given is:
0.2 +0.22 + 0.222 + ... + 0.2222222222
The first term a is 0.2.

To identify the common ratio r, we observe how each term is derived from the previous one. By adding another '2' at the end, we are essentially multiplying by 1.1 (e.g., 0.2 × 1.1 = 0.22, 0.22 × 1.1 = 0.222, and so on).

For a finite geometric series with n terms, the sum S_n is given by:

$$S_n = a\frac{1-r^n}{1-r}$$

Here, a = 0.2, r = 1.1, and n = 10. Now, we'll calculate the sum using these values.

$$S_n = 0.2 \frac{1 - 1.1^{10}}{1 - 1.1}$$

When rounded to the nearest hundredth as per the instruction, the sum of the series is 3.19.

Correct Answer: D

12)   Find the missing number in the box.

$2 \times \square \div (4 \times 3) - 2 = 50$

A) 300   B) 310   C)312   D)320

Solution:

$2 \times \square \div 12 = 52$

$\square \div 12 = 26$

$\square = 26 \times 12$

$\square = 312$

Correct Answer: C

1) What number is 15 more than the greatest whole number less than 50?

A) 64   B) 65   C) 66   D) 67

Solution:

The greatest whole number less than 50 is 49. Adding 15 to 49 gives us 49 + 15 = 64.

Correct Answer: A

2) What number is the sum of 40 + 40 + 40 equal to each of the following except?

A) 60 + 60   B) 50 + 70   C) 30 + 30 + 30 + 30   D) 20 + 20 + 20 + 20 + 20

Solution:
First, we calculate the sum of 40 + 40 + 40, which is 120.
Now we check each option to see which one does not equal 120.
A) 60 + 60 = 120   B) 50 + 70 = 120
C) 30 + 30 + 30 + 30 = 120   D) 20 + 20 + 20 + 20 + 20 = 100
The correct answer is D Because it sums to 100, not 120

Correct Answer: D

3) If I have 5 more than 4 dozen cookies, how many cookies do I have?

A) 53 B) 54 C) 58 D) 60

Solution:
First, we calculate the number of cookies in 4 dozen. Since one dozen is equal to 12, 4 dozen is
$4 \times 12 = 48$.
Next, we add the 5 additional cookies to the 48. So, 48 + 5 = 53.

Correct Answer: A

4) What is the largest whole number less than 50 that is a multiple of 7?

A) 42   B) 45   C) 47   D) 49

Solution:
To solve this, we need to find the multiples of 7 that are less than 50. The largest multiple of 7 less than 50 is 49 (because 7 x 7 = 49, and the next multiple, 7 x 8 = 56, is greater than 50).

Correct Answer: D

5) 5) Juan's 8th birthday will be in 2010. His 12th birthday will be in what year?

A) 2012   B) 2014   C) 2015 D   ) 2016

Solution:
To find out when Juan's 12th birthday is, we add 4 years to the year of his 8th birthday since 12 - 8 = 4.
2010 + 4 = 2014
So, Juan's 12th birthday will be in the year 2014.

Correct Answer: B

6) A gardener planted 2 trees on the first day. If he plants twice as many trees each day as the day before, how many trees will he plant 3 days from the first day?

A) 8   B) 12   C) 16   D) 24

Solution:

The gardener plants twice as many trees each day as the day before, which means the number of trees planted each day forms a geometric sequence with a common ratio of 2.
On the first day, 2 trees are planted. On the second day, 2×2=4 trees are planted. On the third

day, 4×2=8 trees are planted. On the fourth day, 8×2=16 trees are planted.

Therefore, 3 days from the first day (which is the fourth day), the gardener will plant 16 trees.

Correct Answer: C

7) The tens' digit of the product 5678×2345 is?

A) 1   B) 2   C) 7   D) 0

Solution:

we do not need to compute the entire multiplication because we're only interested in one specific digit place – the tens' place.

1. the tens and units digits are 78 and 45 respectively.
2. **Multiply these digits:** Calculate 78×45.
3. **Identify the tens' digit:** From the multiplication 78×45, the tens' digit is 1.

Correct Answer: A

8) Sara turned 8 years old four months ago. Sara will turn 11 years old in months.

A) 28   B) 32   C) 36   D) 40

Solution:

Sara turned 8 years old four months ago, so in 8 months she will turn 9 years old. From her 9th birthday, she needs two more years to turn 11. Two years is 24 months. So, the total months until Sara turns 11 are:

8 months (to turn 9) + 24 months (to turn 11) = 32 months.

Correct Answer: B

9) What is the correct time exactly 50 minutes after 11:00 AM?

A) 11:50 AM   B) 12:00 PM   C) 11:40 AM D)   12:10 PM

Solution:

Starting at 11:00 AM, if we add 50 minutes, we stay within the same hour until we reach 11:59 AM. After that, one more minute would take us to the next hour, which is 12:00 PM. However, since we are only adding 50 minutes, we don't reach the next hour.

11:00 AM + 50 minutes = 11:50 AM.

Correct Answer: A

10) The librarian is 15 years older than my sister, who is three times my age. If I am 7, how old is the librarian?"

A) 36   B) 42   C) 45   D) 51

Solution:

First, we find out how old my sister is by tripling my age: 7 years × 3 = 21 years.

Next, we determine the age of the librarian by adding 15 years to my sister's age: 21 years + 15 years = 36 years.

Correct Answer: A

11) To compute the square of a number, just multiply the number by itself. What is the square of 13?"

A) 100   B) 120   C) 144   D) 169

Solution:

The square of a number is obtained by multiplying the number by itself. So, the square of 8 is 13×13, which is 169.

Correct Answer: D

12) At the book donation event, my group donated 7 books for every 2 books your group donated. If your group donated 28 books, then my group donated ? books.

A) 49 B) 98 C) 77 D) 56

Solution:

If for every 2 books your group donates, my group donates 7, we have a ratio of 7:2. To find out how many books my group donated, we calculate:

Number of books donated by my group = $\frac{7}{2}$ × number of books donated by your group

Plugging in the numbers:
Number of books donated by my group = $\frac{7}{2}$ × 28
Number of books donated by my group = 7 × 14
Number of books donated by my group = 98

Correct Answer: B

1) Determine the smallest fraction from the following group ($\frac{1}{6}$, $\frac{1}{7}$, $\frac{1}{8}$, $\frac{1}{9}$, $\frac{1}{11}$)

A) $\frac{1}{6}$ B) $\frac{1}{7}$ C) $\frac{1}{8}$ D) $\frac{1}{11}$

Solution:

To find the smallest fraction out of a set of fractions with numerators of 1, we need to look for the fraction with the largest denominator because the greater the denominator, the smaller the fraction part.

Given the fractions $\frac{1}{6}$, $\frac{1}{7}$, $\frac{1}{8}$, $\frac{1}{9}$, $\frac{1}{11}$, we can see that $\frac{1}{11}$ has the largest denominator. Hence, $\frac{1}{11}$ is the smallest fraction.

Correct Answer: D

2) Which of the following is equal to $\frac{45}{75}$?

A) 6:10   B) 5:8   C) 9:15   D) 3:5

Solution:

To find a ratio that is equivalent to $\frac{45}{75}$, we can simplify the fraction by dividing the numerator and the denominator by their greatest common divisor (GCD). In this case, the GCD of 45 and 75 is 15.

So, $\frac{45 \div 15}{75 \div 15} = \frac{3}{5}$

Therefore, $\frac{45}{75}$ simplifies to $\frac{3}{5}$.

Correct Answer: D

3) The ratio of boys to girls at Newton Public School is 5: 6. If there are 150 boys at the school, then how many students are there at the school?

A)180   B) 300   C) 330   D) 360

Solution:

The ratio of boys to girls at Newton Public School is given as 5: 6. This means that for every 5 boys, there are 6 girls.

If there are 150 boys, we first find how many times the number of boys is larger than the ratio number for boys. Since $150 \div 5 = 30$, we have 30 times as many boys.

To find the total number of girls, we multiply the ratio number for girls by this same factor of 30: $6 \times 30 = 180$ girls.

To find the total number of students, we add the number of boys and girls together: 150 boys + 180 girls = 330 students.

Correct Answer: C

4) A set of five different positive integers has a mean of 22 and a median of 22. What is the smallest possible integer in the set?

A) 18   B) 20   C) 22   D) 24

Solution:

The mean of the set is 22, so the sum of the five integers is $5 \times 22 = 110$.

The median of the set is 22, which means the third number in the ordered set is 22.

To minimize the smallest integer, we maximize the other numbers. Let's assume the two numbers higher than the median are just above 22, such as 23 and 24. Then the sum of the last two numbers (including the median) is 22 + 23 + 24 = 69.

Subtract this from the total sum to find the sum of the first two numbers: 110 - 69 = 41.

The smallest possible integers that are different positive integers and add up to 41 while being less than the median are 20 and 21,

Therefore, the smallest possible integer in the set is 20.

Correct Answer: B

5) A test has four questions with each question worth one mark. If 10% of the students got O questions correct, 20% got 1 question correct, 30% got 2 questions correct, 25% got 3 questions correct, and 15% got all 4 questions correct, then what was the overall class mean mark?

A) 2.0   B) 2.2   C) 2.5   D) 2.8

Solution:

To calculate the overall class mean mark, we multiply the number of questions correct by the percentage of students that scored those marks, then sum these products.

- 10% of students got O questions correct, contributing 0 x 0.10 = 0 to the mean.
- 20% of students got 1 question correct, contributing 1 x 0.20 = 0.20 to the mean.
- 30% of students got 2 questions correct, contributing 2 × 0.30 = 0.60 to the mean.
- 25% of students got 3 questions correct, contributing 3 x 0.25 = 0.75 to the mean.
- 15% of students got 4 questions correct, contributing 4 × 0.15 = 0.60 to the mean.

Now we add these contributions to find the overall mean:

0+ 0.20 +0.60 +0.75 +0.60 = 2.15

Since we can't have a mean score with a fraction of a mark that isn't accounted for in the options, and the options are in increments of 0.2, we round to the nearest option.

Correct Answer: B

6) Calculate the sum: 2 + 4 + 6 + ... + 98 + 100.

A) 2550 B) 2600 C) 5050 D) 2552

Solution:

The series given is an arithmetic sequence with the first term $a_1 = 2$, the common difference $d = 2$, and the last term $a_n = 100$.

First, let's find the number of terms n in the series. We can use the formula for the nth term of an arithmetic series:

$$a_n = a_1 + (n - 1)d$$

Rearranging to solve for n:

$$n = \frac{(an - a1)}{d} + 1$$

Substituting the given values:

$$n = \frac{(100 - 2)}{2} + 1 = 50$$

There are 50 terms in the series. Now, to find the sum S of an arithmetic series, we can use the formula:

$$S = \frac{n}{2} 2(a_1 + a_n)$$

Substituting the known values:

$$S = 50 (2 + 100) = 25 \times 102 = 2550$$

Correct Answer: A

7) The value of $\dfrac{1}{3-\dfrac{1}{3-\dfrac{1}{3}}}$ is equal to _______.

A) $\dfrac{1}{2}$
B) $\dfrac{2}{3}$
C) $\dfrac{3}{4}$
D) $\dfrac{8}{21}$

Solution:

$$\dfrac{1}{3-\dfrac{1}{3-\dfrac{1}{3}}} = \dfrac{1}{3-\dfrac{1}{\dfrac{8}{3}}} = \dfrac{1}{3-\dfrac{3}{8}} = \dfrac{1}{\dfrac{24}{8}-\dfrac{3}{8}} = \dfrac{1}{\dfrac{21}{8}} = \dfrac{8}{21}$$

Correct Answer: D

8) When you multiply Jane's age and Alex's age, you get 24. If you add their ages together, you get 10. Jane is older than Alex. How old is Alex?

A) 6
B) 4
C) 2
D) 3

Solution:

Let's denote Jane's age by J and Alex's age by A.

1. The product of their ages is 24: J × A = 24
2. The sum of their ages is 10: J+ A = 10
3. Jane is older than Alex, so J > A.

The factors of 24 that add up to 10 are 4 and 6. Since Jane is older, she must be 6 and Alex must be 4.

Correct Answer: B

9) The sum of the digits of all positive primes less than 10 is

A) 17   B) 10   C) 8   D) 4

Solution:

The prime numbers less than 10 are 2, 3, 5, and 7. Adding up all of their digits (2+3+5+7), we get a sum of 17.

Correct Answer: A

10) Of the following, which is between $\frac{1}{4}$ and $\frac{2}{3}$?

A) 0.3   B) 0.5   C) 0.7   D) 0.9

Solution:

First, we need to find the decimal equivalents of $\frac{1}{4}$ and $\frac{2}{3}$.
$\frac{1}{4}$ as a decimal is 0.25.
$\frac{2}{3}$ as a decimal is approximately 0.67.

Now, let's compare these to the options provided:

A) 0.3 is greater than 0.25 but less than 0.67.
B) 0.5 is also greater than 0.25 but less than 0.67.
C) 0.7 is greater than 0.67, so it's not between $\frac{1}{4}$ and $\frac{2}{3}$.
D) 0.9 is also greater than 0.67.

Correct Answer: B

11) If 4 out of 6 teachers recommend reading fiction, what percent do not recommend reading fiction?

A) 25%   B) 33%   C) 50%   D) 66%

Solution:

Out of 6 teachers, if 4 recommend reading fiction, then 6-4 = 2 teachers do not.

To find the percentage of teachers who do not recommend reading fiction, divide the number of teachers who do not recommend by the total number of teachers, and then multiply by 100:

$\frac{2}{6} \times 100 = 33.33\%$

Since we're looking for the closest percentage, we can round this number to the nearest whole number.

Correct Answer: B

12) Michael scored 85, 90, 87, 80, and 92 on his science tests. He has to take one more test. What is the lowest score Michael can earn on his last test and still achieve a mean of at least 86?

A) 80   B) 81   C) 82   D) 95

Solution:

To find the lowest score Michael needs on the last test to have an average (mean) of at least 86:

1. Add his current scores: 85 + 90 + 87 + 80 + 92 = 434
2. Since he will have taken 6 tests, the total score needed for an average of 86: 6 × 86 = 516
3. Subtract his current total from the needed total: 516 - 434 = 82

Correct Answer: C

1) What is the greatest common factor of 36 and 48?

A) 6   B) 12   C) 18   D) 24

Solution:
- Factor 36: 1,2,3,4,6,9,12,18,361,2,3,4,6,9,12,18,36
- Factor 48: 1,2,3,4,6,8,12,16,24,481,2,3,4,6,8,12,16,24,48
- The highest number that is common in both sets is 12.

Correct Answer: B

2) If $\frac{1}{2}$ of a number is 3, what is $\frac{1}{4}$ of the same number?

A) 1.5   B) 6   C) 12   D) 3

Solution:
- Let the number be x. If $\frac{1}{2}x = 3$, then $x = 6$
- $\frac{1}{4}x = \frac{1}{4} \times 6 = 1.5$

Correct Answer: A

3) Which shape has exactly four right angles?

A) Triangle   B) Circle   C) Rectangle   D) Trapezoid

Solution:

A rectangle has exactly four right angles.

Correct Answer: C

4) Sarah has 12 apples. If she gives away 1/3 of her apples, how many does she have left?

A) 4 $\qquad$ B) 8 $\qquad$ C) 16 $\qquad$ D) 9

Solution:

- $\frac{1}{3}$ of 12 apples is 4. If she gives away 4, she has 12 - 4 = 8 apples left

Correct Answer: B

5) If a triangle has angles of 35° and 65°, what is the measure of the third angle?

A) 80° $\qquad$ B) 85° $\qquad$ C) 90° $\qquad$ D) 100°

Solution:

The sum of angles in a triangle is always 180°.

180°-(35°+ 65°) = 180°-100° = 80°

Correct Answer: A

6) What is the median of the set of numbers 4, 8, 6, 10, and 2?

A) 2 $\qquad$ B) 4 $\qquad$ C) 6 $\qquad$ D) 8

Solution:

Arrange the numbers in ascending order: 2, 4, 6, 8, 10. The median is the middle number, which is 6.

Correct Answer: C

7) If you divide a number by 2 and subtract 5, the result is 3. What is the original number?

A) 10   B) 16   C) 18   D) 20

Solution:

- Set up the equation: $\frac{x}{2} - 5 = 3$
- Solve for x: $\frac{x}{2} = 8$ and $x = 16$

Correct Answer: B

8) What is the result of $(3x^2 - 2x + 5) + (x^2 + x - 3)$?

A) $4x^2 - x + 2$ B) $4x^2 - 3x + 8$ C) $4x^2 + x + 2$ D) $3x^2 + x + 2$

Solution:

- Combine like terms: $3x^2 + x2 = 4x^2$, $-2x + x = -x$, and $5-3=2$.
- Simplified expression: $4x^2 \, x + 2$.

Correct Answer: A

9) What is the probability of rolling an even number on a six-sided die?

A) $\frac{1}{6}$ B) $\frac{1}{3}$ C) $\frac{1}{2}$ D) $\frac{2}{3}$

Solution:

There are three even numbers on a six-sided die (2, 4, 6).
The probability is $\frac{3}{6} = \frac{1}{2}$.

Correct Answer: C

10) Convert 0.625 to a fraction.

A) $\frac{5}{8}$ B) $\frac{5}{16}$ C) $\frac{5}{4}$ D) $\frac{3}{5}$

Solution:

- $0.625 = \frac{625}{1000} = \frac{5}{8}$ after simplification.

Correct Answer: A

11) The ratio of boys to girls in a class is 3:4. If there are 12 boys, how many girls are there?

A) 12   B) 14   C) 16   D) 18

Solution:

- If the ratio of boys to girls is 3:4, for every 3 boys, there are 4 girls.
- If there are 12 boys, then $\frac{12}{3} \times 4 = 16$ girls.

Correct Answer: C

12) A tank can be filled by one pipe in 4 hours and by another pipe in 6 hours. How long will it take for both pipes working together to fill the tank?

A) 2.4 hours   B) 2.5 hours   C) 3.0 hours   D) 3.5 hours

Solution:

- The rate of the first pipe is $\frac{1}{4}$ tank/hour, and the second pipe is $\frac{1}{6}$ tank/hour.
- Combined, they fill $\frac{1}{4} + \frac{1}{6} = \frac{5}{12}$ tank/hour.
- It takes $\frac{1}{\frac{5}{12}} = 2.4$ hours to fill the tank.

Correct Answer: A

1) A sequence of numbers begins with 1, 1, 2, 3, 5, 8. What is the next number in this Fibonacci sequence?

A) 10   B) 11   C) 12   D) 13

Solution:
Each number in the sequence is the sum of the two preceding ones. The next number after 5 and 8 is 5+ 8 = 13.

Correct Answer: D

2) Two trains start from the same place and run in opposite directions. One goes west at 60 km/h and the other east at 70 km/h. How far apart are they after 2 hours?

A) 100 km   B) 200 km   C) 260 km   D) 140 km

Solution:
In one hour, the trains are 60km + 70km = 130km apart. In two hours, 130km × 2 = 260km apart.

Correct Answer: C

3) If "MATH" is coded as "NZUI", which word is coded as "BQQMF"?

A) APPLE   B) ANNOY   C) ALONE   D) APART

Solution:
Each letter in "MATH" is shifted by one position in the alphabet to form "NZUI". Applying the reverse to "BQQMF" means shifting each letter back by one, resulting in "APPLE".

Correct Answer: A

4) A clock shows the time as 3:15. What is the angle between the hour and minute hands?

A) 7.5 degrees   B) 97.5 degreesC) 187.5 degrees   D) 277.5 degrees

Solution:
At 3:00, the hour hand is at 90 degrees. Each minute
moves the minute hand by 6 degrees and the hour hand by 0.5 degrees. At 3:15, the minute
hand is at 90 degrees, and the hour hand moves to 97.5 degrees. The difference is 7.5 degrees.

Correct Answer: A

5) An encrypted message uses the following rule: each letter is replaced by the letter three positions down the alphabet. What does the coded message "KHOOR" decode to?

A) HELLO   B) GOODBYE   C) THERE   D) WHERE

Solution:
Decoding "KHOOR" by shifting each letter three positions up the alphabet: K to H, H to E, O to
L, O to L, R to O, results in "HELLO".

Correct Answer: A

6) A drawer contains 12 socks, each one of either black or white. If there are exactly 4 black socks, how many pairs of white socks are there?

A) 2   B) 3   C) 4   D) 5

Solution:

If there are 4 black socks, then there are $12 - 4 = 8$ white socks. A pair consists of 2 socks, so
there are $8/2 = 4$ pairs of white socks.

Correct Answer: C

7) In a family of 6 members P, Q, R, S, T, and U, there are two married couples. T is a teacher and the father of R. U is the grandfather of R and is a lawyer. Q is the bank manager and is married to P. P is not the mother of R. How is S related to U?

A) Daughter   B) Son   C) Daughter-in-law   D) Son-in-law

Solution:

Since U is the grandfather of R and T is the father of R, T's spouse must be R's mother. Since P is not the mother, S must be R's mother and T's wife. U is T's father and S's father-in-law.

Correct Answer: C

8) A bag contains red, blue, and green marbles. There are twice as many blue marbles as red marbles and three times as many green marbles as blue marbles. If there are 5 red marbles, how many marbles are there in total?

A) 45   B) 55   C) 60   D) 65

Solution:

1. Calculate the number of blue marbles:
•Since there are twice as many blue marbles as red marbles, and there are 5 red marbles, there are 2 x 5 = 10 blue marbles.

2. Calculate the number of green marbles:
•Since there are three times as many green marbles as blue marbles, and there are 10 blue marbles, there are 3 x 10 = 30 green marbles.

3. Calculate the total number of marbles:
Adding up all the marbles, we get 5 (red) + 10 (blue) + 30 (green) = 45 marbles in total.

Correct Answer: A

9) The product of two consecutive numbers is 56. What is the smaller number?

A) 6   B) 7   C) 8   D) 9

Solution:

Let the numbers be n and $n + 1$. Then $n(n + 1) = 56$. Solving, $n^2 + n - 56 = 0$. Factorizing, we get $n = 7$ or $n = -8$, so the smaller positive number is 7.

Correct Answer: B

10) If the area of a square is 64 cm2, what is the length of one side?

A) 6 cm   B) 7 cm   C) 8 cm   D) 9 cm

Solution:

The area of a square is given by $side^2$. Thus, $side = \sqrt{64} = 8$ cm.

Correct Answer: C

11) If $x + 3 = 10$, then what is x^2?

A) 49   B) 36   C) 25   D) 16

Solution:

Solving for x, we find $x = 7$. Therefore, $x^2 = 7^2 = 49$

Correct Answer: A

12) A rectangle has a length of 10 cm more than its width. If the width is 5 cm, what is the area?

A) 150 cm2   B) 100 cm2   C) 75 cm2   D) 50 cm2

Solution:

The length is 5 cm + 10 cm = 15 cm. Area = width x length = 5 cm x 15 cm = 75 cm2.

Correct Answer: C

1) Anna thinks of a number, multiplies it by 3, and then subtracts 7. The result is 20. What was the original number?

A) 9   B) 8   C) 10   D) 11

Solution:
Set up the equation based on the problem statement:
3x - 7 = 20. Solving for x, add 7 to both sides to get 3x = 27, then divide by 3 to find x = 9.

Correct Answer: A

2) If five times a number minus two is 48, what is the number?

A) 10   B) 9   C) 8   D) 12

Solution:
Represent the number as x. I ne equation is 5x - 2 = 48. Solve for x by adding 2 to both sides, resulting in 5x = 50, then divide by 5 to get x =10.

Correct Answer: A

3) A farmer wants to fence a rectangular area using 300 meters of fencing. If the length is twice the width, what is the area of the rectangle?

A) 1333 sq m   B) 2000 sq m   C) 2666 sq m   D) 5000 sq m

Solution:
The length is twice the width: $l = 2w$
2. The perimeter P, which is the sum of all sides, is 300 meters: $P = 2l + 2w = 300$
Substituting the first equation into the second gives us: $2(2w) + 2w = 300$
This simplifies to: 4w+2w = 300, 6w = 300 and w = 50 meters
Area=$l \times w$

We found the width (w) of the rectangle to be 50 meters.
Using the relationship that the length (l) is twice the width, the length is 100 meters. The area

(A) of the rectangle is then l X w = 100 × 50 = 5000 square meters. Therefore, the area of the rectangle is 5000 square meters.

Correct Answer: D

4) What fraction is halfway between 1/4 and 3/4?

A) 1/2   B) 1/3   C) 2/5   D) 3/8

Solution:

To find the fraction halfway between 1/4 and 3/4, calculate the average: $\frac{1/4 + 3/4}{2} = \frac{4/4}{2}$ = 1/2.

Correct Answer: A

5) Find the smallest number that is divisible by both 5 and 6.

A) 10   B) 15   C) 30   D) 60

Solution:

The smallest number divisible by both 5 and 6 is their least common multiple (LCM). The LCM of 5 and 6 is 30.

Correct Answer: C

6) If you multiply a number by 3 and then subtract 7, the result is 20. What is the number?

A) 7   B) 8   C) 9   D) 10

Solution:

Set up the equation based on the problem: 3x-7= 20. Solving for x, 3x = 27, So x = 9.

Correct Answer: C

7) What is the result when you multiply the largest single-digit number by the smallest two-digit number?

A) 81	B) 90	C) 100	D) 110

Solution:
The largest single-digit number is 9 and the smallest two-digit number is 10. Multiplying these gives 9 x 10 = 90.

Correct Answer: B

8) If you divide a number by 2 and add 5, the result is 11. What was the original number?

A) 8	B) 10	C) 12	D) 14

Solution:
Let x be the original number. Then, $\frac{n}{2}$ + 5 = 11. Solving for x, subtract 5 from both sides to get $\frac{n}{2}$ = 6, then multiply by 2 to find x = 12.

Correct Answer: C

9) If the sum of two consecutive odd numbers is 56, what is the larger number?

A) 27	B) 29	C) 28	D) 30

Solution:
Let the smaller number be n. The next consecutive odd number is n + 2. The equation n + (n + 2) = 56 simplifies to 2n + 2 = 56, so 2n = 54 and n = 27. Thus, the larger number is 27+ 2 = 29.

Correct Answer: B

10) If five times a number decreased by 2 is 48, what is the number?

A) 8   B) 9   C) 10   D) 11

Solution:
Setting up the equation, 5n — 2 = 48. Adding 2 to both sides gives 5n = 50, and dividing by 5 gives n = 10.

Correct Answer: C

11) The diagonal of a square is 10 cm. Find the area of the square.

A) 50 cm²   B) 75cm²   C) 100 cm²   D) 125cm²

Solution:
The formula relating the side length s of a square to its diagonal d is $d = s\sqrt{2}$
Solving for s, $s = \dfrac{10}{\sqrt{2}} = 5\sqrt{2}$. The area $s^2 = (5\sqrt{2})^2 = 50$ cm².

Correct Answer: A

12) What is the probability of rolling an even number or a number greater than 3 on a standard six-sided die?

A) 1/3   B) 1/2   C) 2/3   D) 5/6

Solution:
The favorable outcomes are 2, 4, 5, 6. That is four out of six possible outcomes, making the probability 4/6 = 2/3.

Correct Answer: C

1) A train travels from Station A to Station B in 3 hours at a speed of 60 km/h. On the return journey, it travels at a speed of 80 km/h. How long does the return journey take?

A) 2.25 hours   B) 2.5 hours   C) 2.75 hours   D) 3 hours

Solution:

The distance between Station A and Station B can be found using the speed and time of the outward journey:

$$Distance = Speed \times Time = 60 \, km/h \times 3 \, h = 180 \, km$$

For the return journey, using the same distance and the speed of 80 km/h:

$$Time = \frac{Distance}{Speed} = \frac{180 \, km}{80 \, km/h} = 2.25 \, hours$$

Correct Answer: A

2) A rectangular field is twice as long as it is wide. If the perimeter of the field is 180 meters, what are the field's dimensions?

A) 40m by 30m   B) 45m by 90m   C) 40m by 80m   D) 30m by 60m

Solution:

Let the width of the field be w meters. Then, its length is 2w meters. The perimeter of a rectangle is given by 2(length + width):

2(2w+w) = 180

6w=180

w= 30 meters

So, the length is 2w = 60 meters.

Correct Answer: D

3) If five pencils cost as much as three erasers, and one eraser costs 40 cents, how much do two pencils cost?

A) 24 cents   B) 48 cents   C) 60 cents   D) 80 cents

Solution:
First, find the cost of one eraser: 40 cents. Since five pencils cost the same as three erasers:
3 x 40 cents = 5 x pencil cost
120 cents = 5 x pencil cost
1 x pencil cost = 24 cents

Therefore, two pencils cost:
2 x 24 cents = 48 cents

Correct Answer: B

4) Leo has some stickers. If he gives 5 stickers to each of his 4 friends, he will have 7 stickers left. How many stickers does Leo have?

A) 27   B) 28   C) 29   D) 30

Solution:
If Leo gives 5 stickers to each of his 4 friends, he gives away a total of 5 x 4 = 20 stickers.

After giving the stickers away, he has 7 left. So the total number of stickers he had was 20+ 7 = 27.

Correct Answer: A

5) The sum of three consecutive even numbers is 48. What is the smallest of these numbers?

A) 14   B) 12   C) 16   D) 10

Solution:

Let the smallest even number be n. The next two consecutive even numbers would be n+2 and n + 4.

Their sum is n + (n + 2) + (n + 4) = 48:

3n+6=48

3n= 42

n = 14

So the smallest of the three numbers is 14.

Correct Answer: A

6) What is the value of the expression $5^2 - (3^3 - 2^2)$?

A) 2   B) 8   C) 10   D) 16

Solution:

First, calculate the power of 3 and 2:

$3^3 = 3 \times 3 \times 3 = 27$

$2^2 = 2 \times 2 = 4$

Then perform the subtraction inside the parentheses:

$3^2 - 2^2 = 27 - 4 = 23$

Now, calculate the power of 5:

$5^2 = 5 \times 5 = 25$

Finally, subtract the result from the parentheses from 5^2:

$5^2 - (3^3 - 2^2) = 25 - 23 = 2$

So, the value of the expression is 2.

Correct Answer: A

7) 3.982 =

A. three and ninety-eight hundredths
B. thirty-nine and eighty-two hundredths
C. three and nine hundred eighty-two thousandths
D. three and ninety-two hundredths

Solution:

To solve this, we need to correctly interpret the decimal number 3.982:
• The digit "3" is in the ones place, indicating the whole number part.
• The digits "982" after the decimal point represent the fractional part. In this case, "982" stands for nine hundred eighty-two thousandths because the last digit is in the thousandths place. Therefore, 3.982 can be read as "three and nine hundred eighty-two thousandths," making the

Correct Answer: C

8) What is the nearest integer to 2.49?

A) 2   B) 3   C) 2.5   D) 2.4

Solution:

The nearest integer to 2.49, following the standard rounding rules, is 2. This is because the decimal part, .49, is less than 0.5, leading us to round down to the nearest whole number. Therefore, the correct answer to the similar question is A.

Correct Answer: A

9) A square lawn has a side length of 40 meters. A flowerbed is planned to be built along one edge of the lawn, running the entire length of that edge, and covering 10% of the lawn's total area. What will be the width of the flowerbed?

A. 1 meter   B. 2 meters   C. 4 meters   D. 10 meters

Solution:

1. Total Area of the Lawn: The area of a square is given by the formula side2. So, for the lawn, Area 40 m x 40 m = 1600 m2.

2. Area Covered by the Flowerbed: The flowerbed covers 10% of the lawn's total area, Flowerbed Area = 1600 m2 x 0.10 = 160 m2.

3. Determining the Width of the Flowerbed:

• Since the flowerbed runs along one edge of the square lawn, its length is equal to one side of the lawn, 40 meters.

• Let w be the width of the flowerbed. The area of the flowerbed can also be calculated as length x width,

40 m X w = 160 m2.

Solving for w gives us the width of the flowerbed. Let's calculate it directly.
The width of the flowerbed, which covers 10% of the square lawn's total area, can be calculated by dividing the area of the flowerbed by the length of one side of the lawn. Given that the flowerbed's area is 160 m2 and it runs along one edge of the lawn (40 meters in length), the width of the flowerbed is:

$$w = \frac{160\ m^2}{40\ m} = 40\ m$$

Therefore, the width of the flowerbed is **4 meters,**

Correct Answer: C

10) Simplify the expression: $(2^4)^3 \times 2^5$.

A) 2^{17} B) 2^{20} C) 2^{23} D) 2^{32}

Solution:

To simplify the expression $(2^4)^3 \times 2^5$., we apply the rule of exponents which states that $(a^m)^n = a^{m \times n}$

So, $(2^4)^3 = 2^{4 \times 3} = 2^{12}$

Now, multiplying 2^{12} by 2^5, we add the exponents: $12 + 5 = 17$.

Therefore, the expression simplifies to 2^{17}.

Correct Answer: A

11) Which of the following numbers is divisible by both 4 and 9?

A) 81   B) 126   C) 144   D) 190

Solution:

To be divisible by both 4 and 9, the number must be divisible by 4 x 9 = 36, which is their least common multiple.

Among the given options, only 144 is divisible by 36 (36 × 4 = 144).

Correct Answer: C

12) If $\frac{2}{3}$ of a cake is eaten, and then $\frac{3}{4}$ of the remaining cake is eaten, what fraction of the original cake is left?

A) $\frac{1}{3}$ B) $\frac{1}{4}$ C) $\frac{1}{6}$ D) $\frac{1}{12}$

Solution:

If $\frac{2}{3}$ of a cake is eaten, then $\frac{1}{3}$ of it remains.

If $\frac{3}{4}$ of the remaining cake is eaten, then $\frac{1}{4}$ of it remains.

So, the fraction of the original cake that is left is $\frac{1}{3} \times \frac{1}{4} = \frac{1}{12}$

Correct Answer: D

1) A car travels at a constant speed of 60 miles per hour. How many miles will the car travel in 2.5 hours?

A) 120 miles   B) 150 miles   C) 180 miles   D) 200 miles

Solution:

To find out how many miles the car will travel in 2.5 hours, we multiply the speed (60 miles per hour) by the time (2.5 hours):

Distance = Speed × Time

Distance = 60 miles/hour × 2.5 hours

Distance = 150 miles

Correct Answer: B

2) Ten years ago, Alice was twice as old as her brother. If Alice is currently 30 years old, how old is her brother?

A) 10 years   B) 15 years   C) 20 years   D) 25 years

Solution:

Let's represent Alice's age 10 years ago as A and her brother's age 10 years ago as B. According to the given information, ten years ago, Alice was twice as old as her brother, so we can write:

A = 2B

Given that Alice is currently 30 years old, we can find her age 10 years ago:

A = 30 - 10

A = 20

Now, we can use this information to find her brother's age 10 years ago:

20 = 2B

B =20/2

B = 10

So, her brother's age 10 years ago was 10 years.

To find his current age, we add 10 years:

Brother's current age = 10 + 10 = 20

Therefore, Alice's brother is currently 20 years old.

Correct Answer: C

3) Solve the following two-step equation involving fractions:

$$\frac{3}{4}x - \frac{1}{2} = \frac{5}{8}$$

A) $x = \frac{9}{16}$　　　　B) $x = \frac{7}{8}$　　　　C) $x = \frac{5}{16}$　　　　D) $x = \frac{3}{2}$

Solution:

To solve the equation, we need to isolate x on one side of the equation.

Step 1: Add $\frac{1}{2}$ to both sides of the equation to isolate the term containing X:

$$\frac{3}{4}x - \frac{1}{2} + \frac{1}{2} = \frac{5}{8} + \frac{1}{2}$$

$$\frac{3}{4}x = \frac{5}{8} + \frac{4}{8}$$

$$\frac{3}{4}x = \frac{9}{8}$$

Step 2: Multiply both sides of the equation by the reciprocal of $\frac{3}{4}$, which is $\frac{4}{3}$, to solve for x:

$$\frac{4}{3} \times \frac{3}{4}x = \frac{4}{3} \times \frac{9}{8}$$

$$x = \frac{36}{24}$$

$$x = \frac{3}{2}$$

Therefore, the solution to the equation is $x = \frac{3}{2}$.

Correct Answer: D

4) In a certain pattern, the number of sides in each successive shape increases in the following order: Triangle, Square, Pentagon, Hexagon, ...
Based on the pattern, which shape corresponds to the 8th shape in the sequence?

A) Octagon   B) Nonagon   C) Decagon   D) Dodecagon

Solution:

The sequence of shapes is increasing by one side at each step:
• 1st shape: Triangle (3 sides)
• 2nd shape: Square (4 sides)
• 3rd shape: Pentagon (5 sides)
• 4th shape: Hexagon (6 sides)

Following this pattern, the 8th shape in the sequence would have 3+ 7 = 10 sides, because you add one more side for each step in the sequence from the starting point of a triangle.

Correct Answer: C

5) Anna is twice as old as Ben. The sum of their ages is 36 years. How old will Anna be in 4 years?

A) 20 years   B) 24 years   C) 28 years   D) 32 years

Solution:
Let's denote Anna's current age as A and Ben's current age as B.
The given statements translate to the following equations:
  1. A =2B (Anna is twice as old as Ben)
  2. A + B = 36 (The sum of their ages is 36)

Substituting A from the first equation into the second equation:
2B+ B = 36
3B = 36
B = 12

Now, using B = 12 to find A:

A = 2(12)

A = 24

Anna's current age is 24 years. In 4 years, Anna will be:

24+4 = 28 years old.

Correct Answer: C

6) A car and a motorcycle set off from the same point, traveling in opposite directions. The car travels at a speed of 60 kilometers per hour, and the motorcycle at a speed of 90 kilometers per hour. How far apart will they be after 2 hours?

A) 150 kilometers   B) 180 kilometers   C) 300 kilometers   D) 320 kilometers

Solution:

The distance covered by each vehicle can be calculated using the formula:

$$Distance = Speed \ x \ Time$$

For the car:

$$Distance_{car} = 60 \times 2 = 120 \ kilometers$$

For the motorcycle:

$$Distance_{motorcycle} = 90 \times 2 = 180 \ kilometers$$

Since they are traveling in opposite directions, the total distance between them after 2 hours will be the sum of the individual distances:

$$Total \ Distance = Distance_{car} + Distance_{motorcycle} = 120 + 180 = 300 \ kilometers$$

Correct Answer: C

7) Find the missing number in the following number sequence. 2, 6, 18,_, 162, 486.

A) 54 B) 58 C) 60 D) 64

Solution:
By examining the pattern, we notice that each number is a multiple of the previous one. To find the pattern, let's look at the ratios of successive numbers:

$$\frac{6}{2}=3$$
$$\frac{18}{6}=3$$

It seems that each number is 3 times the previous number. This is a geometric sequence with a common ratio of 3.

So, to find the missing number, we multiply the second number in the sequence by 3:
18*3 = 54
The missing number in the sequence is 54.

Correct Answer: A

8) There are 200 pupils in a school club at first. If the number of boys increases by 10 and the number of girls decreases by 10%, the number of pupils in the club will become 194. How many boys are there in the club at first?

A) 70 B) 100 C) 110 D) 120

Solution:

Let the number of boys be B and the number of girls be G. We know that initially: B+G= 200

After the changes, the number of boys becomes B + 0.1B, and the number of girls becomes G - 0.1G = 0.9G, leading to:
1.1B + 0.9G = 194

Simplify and express G in terms of B: $1.1B + 0.9(200 - B) = 194$

Now solve for B:

$1.1B + 180 - 0.9B = 194$
$0.2B = 14$
$2B = 140$
$B = 70$

Correct Answer: A

9) The sum of two numbers is 160. The sum of of the smaller number and 2 of the greater number is 100. Find the difference between the two numbers.

A) 20   B) 40   C) 60   D) 128

Solution:
Let the smaller number be s and the greater number be g.

We are given two equations:
1. $s + g = 160$ (Equation 1)
2. $\frac{1}{4}s + \frac{2}{3}g = 100$ (Equation 2)

First, let's clear the fractions in Equation 2 by finding a common denominator, which is 12. This gives us:
$3s + 8g = 1200$

Now we have the system of equations:
1. $s + g = 160$
2. $3s + 8g = 1200$

Multiply Equation 1 by 3 to align with Equation 2:
$3s + 3g = 480$ (Equation 3)

Subtract Equation 3 from Equation 2:

$5g = 720$

Now solve for g:

$g = \dfrac{720}{5}$

$9 = 144$

Now find s using Equation 1:

$s + 144 = 160$

$s = 160 - 144$

$s = 16$

The difference between the two numbers is:

$g - s = 144 - 16$

$g - s = 128$

Correct Answer: D

10) Of the whole numbers from 1 through 50, how many are 4 more than another whole number from 1 through 46?

A) 42   B) 46   C)48   D) 51

Solution:

We need to find out how many numbers are exactly 4 greater than another number in the range 1 to 46. The smallest number that is 4 more than a number in this range is 5 (since 1+ 4 = 5), and the largest is 50 (since 46 + 4 = 50).

Thus, every number from 5 through 50 will be 4 more than another number from 1 through 46. That gives us a total of 50 - 5+1 = 46 numbers.

Correct Answer: B

11) My initials are the 5th, 15th, and 19th letters of the alphabet, in that order. My name could be"

A) Edward Oscar Sullivan
B) Erin Olivia Scott
C) Emma Olive Smith
D) Ethan Oliver Sanders

Solution:

The 5th letter of the alphabet is E, the 15th is O, and the 19th is S. Therefore, the initials must be E.O.S.

The name that matches these initials from the options given is C

Correct Answer: C

12) A circumference of a circle is three times as long as a side of a square. If the circumference of the circle is 18, how long is a side of the square?

A) 2 B) 4 C) 6 D) 9

Solution:

The circumference of the circle is given as 18, which is three times the length of a side of the square.

To find the side of the square, we divide the circumference of the circle by 3.

$$\text{Side of the square} = \frac{\text{Circumference of the circle}}{3}$$

$$\text{Side of the square} = \frac{18}{3}$$
$$\text{Side of the square} = 6$$

Therefore, the length of a side of the square is 6.
Correct Answer: C

1) The area of a rectangular garden is $72\frac{1}{2}$ square meters. The length is $14\frac{1}{4}$ meters. What is the width, in meters, of the garden?

A) 5 B) $5\frac{1}{3}$ C) $5\frac{5}{57}$ D) $5\frac{3}{4}$

Solution:

To find the width, we divide the area by the length:

$$Width = \frac{Area}{Length} = \frac{72\frac{1}{2}}{14\frac{1}{4}} = \frac{145}{2} \div \frac{57}{4} = \frac{145}{2} \times \frac{4}{57} = \frac{290}{57}$$

Converting $\frac{290}{57}$ to a mixed number gives us $5\frac{5}{57}$,

Correct Answer: C

2) An outfit consists of a shirt, pants, and an optional jacket. If there are 5 choices of shirts, 4 choices of pants, and 2 choices of jackets (black, white), how many outfits are possible?

A) 30   B) 40   C) 50   D) 60

Solution:

For each shirt and pant combination, there can be no jacket, a black jacket, or a white jacket. So for each combination of shirt and pants, there are 2 jacket choices plus the option of not wearing a jacket, which gives 3 total options for the jacket.

The total number of outfits is calculated by:

Total outfits = (Number of shirts) × (Number of pants) × (Number of jacket options including not wearing one)

Total outfits = 5 x 4 x (2+1)

Total outfits = 5 x 4 x 3

Total outfits = 60

Correct Answer: D

3) Ms. Chen's salary increases by 4 percent each year. If her salary for 2018 was $50,000, what will her salary for 2023 be?

A) $60,832.65   B) $61,665.12   C) $59,270.40   D) $58,235.53

Solution:

Ms. Chen's initial salary for 2018 is $50,000, and it increases by 4% each year. To find her salary for 2023, which is 5 years later:

Final salary = Initial salary × (1+ annual increase rate)^{years}
Final salary = $50000 \times (1+0.04)^5$
Final salary = $50000 \times 1.04^5 = \$60,832.65$

Correct Answer: A

4) If 3 is added to a number and this sum is tripled, the result is 21. What is the number?

A) 2   B) 3   C) 4   D) 5

Solution:
- Let the number be x. Then, $3(x + 3) = 21$.
- Solve: $x + 3 = 7$ and $x = 4$.

Correct Answer: C

5) A rectangle's length is three times its width. If the perimeter is 48 cm, what is the length?

A) 9 cm   B) 12 cm   C) 18 cm   D) 36 cm

Solution:
Let width = w and length = 3w.
Perimeter formula: $2(3w+w) = 48$ leads to
$8w = 48$, so $w = 6$ cm and $3w = 18$ cm.

Correct Answer: C

6) If the sum of three consecutive numbers is 42, what is the smallest number?

A) 12   B) 13   C) 14   D) 15

Solution:

Let the numbers be x, $x + 1$, $x + 2$.

The equation $x + (x + 1) + (x + 2) = 42$ simplifies to

$3x + 3 = 42$, and $x = 13$.

Correct Answer: B

7) In a sequence, the first term is 1 and each successive term is the sum of all previous terms plus 1. What is the fifth term in the sequence?

A) 16   B) 15   C) 31   D) 32

Solution:

The sequence starts with 1. The second term is 1+1=2.

The third term is 1+2+1= 4. The fourth term is 1+2+4+1 = 8. The fifth term is 1+2+4+8+1=16.

Correct Answer: A

8) What is the smallest integer greater than 1 that is both square and a cube?

A) 8   B) 16   C) 64   D) 81

Solution:

The number must be a sixth power since it's the least common multiple of 2 (square) and 3 (cube). The smallest such number is $2^6 = 64$.

Correct Answer: C

9) If the sum of the first n positive integers is 210, what is n?

A) 20   B) 21   C) 19   D) 22

Solution:
The sum of the first n positive integers is given by $\frac{n(n+1)}{2}$ = 210.
Solving for n, n² + n - 420=0. The positive root of this quadratic equation is n = 20.

Correct Answer: A

10) Simplify the expression √50+ √18 - √8.

A)3√2   B) 5√2   C) 6√2   D) 9√2

Solution:
Break each term into prime factors and simplify:
√50 = 5√2,
√18 = 3√2,
√8 = 2√2.
Adding and subtracting gives 5√2 +3√2 − 2√2 = 6√2.

Correct Answer: C

11) A water tank is filled by two pipes. The first pipe alone can fill the tank in 40 minutes, and the second pipe can fill it in 60 minutes. How long will it take for both pipes to fill the tank together?

A) 24 minutes   B) 25 minutes   C) 30 minutes   D) 35 minutes

Solution:
The first pipe fills $\frac{1}{40}$ of the tank per minute, and the second pipe fills $\frac{1}{60}$ of the tank per minute. Together, they fill $\frac{1}{40} + \frac{1}{60} = \frac{3}{120} + \frac{2}{120} = \frac{5}{120} = \frac{1}{24}$ of the tank per minute. Thus, they can fill the tank in 24 minutes.

Correct Answer: A

12) A number consists of two digits whose sum is 9. If the digits are reversed, the new number is 27 less than the original number. What is the original number?

A) 63	B) 54	C) 45	D) 36

Solution:

Let the tens digit be x and the units digit be y. Then
$x + y = 9$ and
$10x + y = 10y + x - 27$.

Simplifying the second equation gives
$9x - 9y = -27$, or $x - y = -3$.

Solving these equations together, $x = 3$ and $y = 6$, so the number is 36.

Correct Answer: D

ANSWER KEYS

Test 1

1	2	3	4	5	6	7	8	9	10	11	12
B	B	A	A	C	A	A	B	D	D	B	A

Test 2

1	2	3	4	5	6	7	8	9	10	11	12
B	B	A	A	A	B	A	C	C	B	A	D

Test 3

1	2	3	4	5	6	7	8	9	10	11	12
C	A	B	A	A	B	B	B	A	B	B	B

Test 4

1	2	3	4	5	6	7	8	9	10	11	12
A	A	B	A	A	B	B	B	B	A	B	A

Test 5

1	2	3	4	5	6	7	8	9	10	11	12
A	B	B	A	B	B	B	A	A	B	B	B

Test 6

1	2	3	4	5	6	7	8	9	10	11	12
C	A	B	A	B	A	C	A	A	A	B	B

Test 7

1	2	3	4	5	6	7	8	9	10	11	12
D	A	A	B	B	C	D	B	D	C	D	C

Test 8

1	2	3	4	5	6	7	8	9	10	11	12
A	D	A	D	B	C	A	B	A	A	D	B

Test 9

1	2	3	4	5	6	7	8	9	10	11	12
D	D	C	B	B	A	D	B	A	B	B	C

Test 10

1	2	3	4	5	6	7	8	9	10	11	12
B	A	C	B	A	C	B	A	C	A	C	A

Test 11

1	2	3	4	5	6	7	8	9	10	11	12
D	C	A	A	A	C	C	A	B	C	A	C

Test 12

1	2	3	4	5	6	7	8	9	10	11	12
A	A	D	A	C	C	B	C	B	C	A	C

ANSWER KEYS

Test 13

1	2	3	4	5	6	7	8	9	10	11	12
A	D	B	A	A	A	C	A	C	A	C	D

Test 14

1	2	3	4	5	6	7	8	9	10	11	12
B	C	D	C	C	C	A	A	D	B	C	C

Test 15

1	2	3	4	5	6	7	8	9	10	11	12
C	D	A	C	C	B	A	C	A	C	A	D